This book is dedicated to every healthcare professional who ever stopped and wondered what the hell they were doing....

Thank you for Dying: A Hospital Memoir

Chapter 1

"Oh that's just God, he thinks he's a Doctor…. or something like that, I always get the punch line wrong."

I smiled politely and did my best to portray some genuine amusement. Being my last day on the psych unit I was admittedly a little touched at my patients attempt to amuse me with an old hospital joke. This type of acting by staff when dealing with a patient considered as dangerous as this one was quite common. There seems to be a direct correlation between the preservation of a patient's pride, and the ability to go home unharmed for the day. The balancing act of course is being able to confront such a patient in a therapeutic way, while keeping that pride, and your face, intact.

A hospital is the apex of human existence, most of us enter this world via hospital, and will likely leave it in one as well. Birth and death it seems are usually only a short elevator ride away from each other. (Although I have seen both take place actually ON an elevator) Everything from the sounds, to the smells, are unique to the hospital environment. Some like to play a cute little lullaby jingle over the intercom system whenever a baby is born, while not a minute later, the sharp contrast of a brash voice with unmistakable urgency can be heard announcing the location of a code blue. People in the various waiting rooms look up from pretending to read their 7yr old doctors office magazine, as if they are going to see a blood covered gurney go racing by like on television.

The smells of course vary by floor. From the overwhelming aroma of stale urine, that can almost take on a fog-like appearance on a geriatric unit, to the almost appealing smell of baby pee coming from the maternity ward. One as conditioned as myself could easily navigate through an entire hospital using my olfactory skills alone to decipher various shades of urine.

A Psychiatric unit, now that is a world of its own. I've actually seen someone *make* a dentist appointment to avoid doing a shift there. It's been said that there are only two kinds of nurses, those that deal with the neck up, and those that deal with the neck down. They rarely switch sides. I generally would rather volunteer for an elective root canal than work a shift on an ICU, however I seem to be in the vast minority.

Something happens to a person when they reach the locked entrance of a psych unit. A built-in alert system seems to kick in to remind you that there is a reason this door is locked. Are they keeping me out, them in, or both? Rest assured, it's both, and your tension level gets an inevitable boost once you pass through that door. Of course, you may first have to speak to someone on the other side either via phone or a fast food style speaker on the wall just to gain access. Once inside, it's as if you just crashed your ex's wedding in a bad 80s movie. The music comes to a screeching halt and everyone stops what they are doing to look at who just came in. In reality, the staff tends to welcome a new face on the unit, and generally feels the need to protect them from any potential mishaps.

The patient's reaction of course varies wildly. Are you a superhero doctor here to rescue them, or a demon that has come to drag them to hell? Perhaps you appear to be Elvis Presley, or their mother. Either way, there are endless possibilities as to how you will be received, but in general, fear not. Contrary to popular belief, it is unlikely that as a visitor any harm will come to you at the hand of a psychiatric patient.

The regular staff however, plays a different role and suffers different consequences. They have the privilege of playing a more permanent role in the life of a psychologically disturbed patient. That can be good or bad, depending on how successfully, and carefully that role is played. Are they stuck being the superhero doctor, or the demon (or Elvis). Either way, a skilled professional should be able to manipulate that appearance into something therapeutic. With the hope of eventually shifting that patient's perception back to a more reasonable place. And for the nonprofessional, this can be a hilarious opportunity to entertain yourself for a 12 hour shift.

Aside from the potential dangers and somewhat shameful entertainment value, a certain type of healthcare professional seems to be attracted to this field. Tragically, its rarely due to a genuine fascination with human behavior, or a desire to help your fellow man. As much as it is for the patients, for staff, a psychiatric unit ends up being a place to hide.

This can occur for many reasons, some as simple as being grossly inept at any other aspect of healthcare. Other reasons tend to stem from the staff themselves being as mentally ill as the patients they care for. Do to the stigma and fear surrounding mental health patients, working on this kind of unit can be the equivalent of living on a desert island.

Another theory, and my personal favorite, is that "crazy" is contagious. If one works in this environment long enough, they just may lose their own grip on reality. Perhaps the constant bombardment of irrational thoughts and perceptions eventually start to penetrate. Some of the more convincing delusional and antisocial patients may start to make sense after spending 8 to 12 of your waking hours with them on a daily basis. Then you can either take a vacation, make an adjustment in your career trajectory, or get a room right next to your new mentor.

Perhaps this is how the more interesting psychiatric patients are born. We tend to wonder 'what happened' whenever that patient being rolled in 4 point restraints has an interesting back story. The former college professor, lawyer, or school nurse that is now rambling incoherently and has been deemed unfit for society by the powers that be. What happened? Was it an unimaginable series of stressful or even tragic events? Maybe a genetic predisposition toward mental illness, or did a crazy person sneeze near them on a crowded elevator? Either way, psychiatric patients love to break the mold and emerge from all walks of life. What makes me love them is their ability to throw curve balls at any established theory, at any given time.

For general descriptive purposes, I have lumped all psychiatric patients into two convenient categories, the funny and the disturbing. We've all seen the ladder make headlines on CNN, from Ted Bundy to Ted Kaczynski. While I have had more than my share of experiences with the disturbing, I prefer to focus on the funny, and sleep better at night. (or during the day, such is the life of an RN)

The funny, of course, is also a matter of opinion. Personally, I have always preferred the patients I find arguing with a coffee mug named Steve, the ones that are compelled to do a cartwheel any time a phone rings, or even the one apprehended after attempting to direct traffic at an intersection dressed as Napoleon Bonaparte.

An all time personal favorite of mine was a man that believed he was God. He was a bit of an ornery old man, white hair with a full beard, maybe something like we would expect God to look like. They would let him watch the religion channel on television. I'm not sure this was entirely therapeutic or even appropriate all things considered, but like many questionable decisions made regarding patient care back then, I went along with it. We would see him watching ever so intently mere inches from the screen, nodding knowingly as the people on the screen spoke, especially when they prayed.

This patient was a bit 'resistant' to medication as they say. In fact he was so resistant that taking any kind of daily medication by mouth was simply not an option, or you would most certainly have a fight on your hands. The solution came in the form of a monthly injection of an antipsychotic medication designed to work over an extended period of time, for just such a situation.

Tensions were high on 'shot days', for both patient and staff. His favorite staff members would be gathered from throughout the building, of all ranks and titles in hopes of keeping him calm for his injection and avoiding any ugly altercations. This plan usually worked, and he would receive his shot without a violent altercation, however the rest of the day would likely consist of threats of floods and other Biblical wraths that only a true deity could be capable of. Once calm, and back at his psychological baseline, he would always apologize for his actions. True remorse could be felt with his words, by his face, and his very presence. He would be moved to tears on occasion. Anytime there was any type of natural disaster on the news, he would become tearful, and apologize, after all they were his fault, for he was God. And on every 'shot day' that I can remember….it rained.

My adventures in behavioral health began in very humble surroundings. My first real job in the field consisted of degrading duties and even more degrading compensation. The bowels of healthcare so to speak, these kinds of positions were usually disguised by lofty job titles such as "Residential Mental Health Technician" or "Day Habilitation Specialist". The fact that the educational requirements for such a position consist of a high school diploma (or equivalent) probably should have been a dead giveaway that this was not necessarily the gateway to a lavish career in medicine. If that was not enough, perhaps the fact that several of my coworkers were either recent parolees, or so disheveled in appearance that if they lost their nametag they may not be allowed to leave, for fear that we may accidently release a newly admitted psych patient.

The facility its self was like something out of a low budget horror movie from the 1960s. That also being the time period when any equipment upgrades or significant maintenance probably took place. The term 'low budget' also seemed key on many levels. In the defense of those who run facilities such as this, it's not their fault, it's ours. The average United States citizen still cringes at the thought of mental illness, most are ashamed, embarrassed or even frightened at the very thought of it affecting someone in their lives. This primitive attitude toward mental illness of course carries over into our political system, and therefore our budgets. Mental health agencies largely depend on state and federal funding. It is by far the lowest priority on the political totem pole, and is funded accordingly. These agencies have to fight for every dime they ever see. Unfortunately money it seems is always the bottom line.

The truly ironic part of all of this is that psychiatry has by a large margin the most successful cure rate of any medical field. Unlike an oncology unit, or ICU, mental health patients are much more likely to report relief from debilitating symptoms, and go home after a hospital stay. In reality, what that means for a hospital, believe it or not, is less money. Under our current system, hospitals don't make a profit if you are home and well. The biggest, most profitable disease currently known to man, is cancer. Cancer keeps hospitals in business. So when a budget committee meets to decide where to invest in its facilities, where do you think the money goes? We have all seen, or at least heard of the grand opening of a new hospital wing or public health clinic with all the new bells and whistles. What we don't see are these kinds of improvements, or even upkeep at a mental health facility. These places remain hidden, in the closet, every hospitals dirty little secret.

This environment is where we attempt to heal the mentally ill in this country. I always thought it was a little, well, 'crazy' for lack of a better term. Sometimes it seems the patient doesn't get better *because* of our best efforts, they get better despite them.

Historically, mental illness has always been something surrounded with hysteria of some kind, blame being pointed at everything from bad blood, to supernatural possession. Anything but a legitimate disease, it seems *that* was too far fetched. The very word "disease" arising from the words "dis" and "ease", originally intended to describe someone who was not at ease. Illness it seems has always been something that can only effect the body. The treatment was often more savage than the disease, in fact the phrase "beat the hell" out of someone, was originally coined from a treatment that consisted of beating a mentally ill patient that was believed to be possessed. The idea was to quite literally beat the evil illness out of them. Despite our ancestors best efforts, these so called treatments were generally quite ineffective.

Some would argue that many of our more modern treatments are not much of an improvement, and they would be right. Many of today's treatment professionals are "prescribers", so they do just that, prescribe. Unfortunately it seems the first line of defense in the war on mental illness is to medicate. (when it should probably be meditate) This is essentially like killing a fly with a sledgehammer. The vast majority of antipsychotic, and even antidepressive medications have the ability to take a moderately disruptive condition, and turn it into a devastating one.

We have all seen the commercials for the latest pharmaceutical masterpiece. A brand new drug that will solve any problem you may have, even some you didn't know you had until this very commercial. They start with some vague innocent question to the viewer, "Do you, or does someone you know, feel tired in the morning?" The unsuspecting viewer thinks, *Hey, I feel tired in the morning sometimes.* Then the commercial spirals the viewer into a virtual panic attack by listing all of the horrible diseases ever associated with fatigue. (which is perhaps the most vague symptom in existence) So now, instead of just being a little tired in the morning, like most working adults, you have herpes, or cancer, or even worse, you can't get a boner! And for a nominal fee, (if you have insurance) they can cure your ailment.

But for those of us that like to read the fine print, or at least pay attention, there is usually a very quick, subtle little 'FYI' at the end of each commercial. This tends to contain some minor little details like "possible side effects". Some so outrageous that the jokes tend to write themselves. "May cause rectal bleeding, infertility, or sudden death!" Oops, I'm sorry, but it sounded like you said *sudden death*? That's right, the medication you have taken to help improve your mood, or enhance your manhood might kill you instead. It has actually happened with enough regularity that they are required to put a disclaimer in the commercial. This should probably scare people more than it does.

People seldom fear the right things. We buy hand sanitizer by the gallon in hopes of warding off the latest media hyped virus, but have no problem reading a text message while driving 70mph on our way to purchase it. We are petrified of speaking in front of a room full of people, but have no problem spewing personal drama to hundreds of them on Facebook or Twitter. The problem with most 'normal' people is that they are just that.... normal.

In general mathematics, the word 'normal' simply refers to a lack of significant deviation from the average. This is a very simple, almost elegant definition of a word that in reality, our culture especially, has developed to a point of almost infinite complexity. Normal, it seems, very much depends on the point of view. To someone like Bill Gates or Warren Buffett it is perfectly normal to take a helicopter to a beach house for the weekend. While to a person in the African country of Ghana, it may be perfectly normal to spend the day in search of food and clean water.

In the somewhat distorted world of healthcare, the word "Normal" can take on a complex range of perspectives. For a patient, things like being stuck with needles, peeing into a bag, and even being 'felt up' by strangers can evolve into a certain level of normalcy. On the other side of that coin of course is the staff. A small army of educated professionals who have somehow convinced themselves that sticking people with needles, carrying a urine sample, or touching a strangers genitals in a well-lit room are as routine as a morning cup of coffee. As the great Austrian Psychiatrist Afred Adler once said, "The only normal people are the ones you don't know very well."

Chapter 2

"A person who never made a mistake never tried anything new."

-Albert Einstein

Normalcy at last, day one on a standard, run of the mill medical floor. No crazy people, just regular doctors, nurses, and patients with broken bones and stomachaches…. said the foolish nurse. In hindsight, a *normal* person probably wouldn't see anything routine or mundane about being anywhere inside of a hospital. Nurses and doctors tend to forget things like that.

Already a sense of change sweeps over me as I realize I just walked on my new unit without having to first pass through any sort of security system. (I'm still trying to figure out if this implies safety, or a lack there of) That 'hospital smell' is a lot more prevalent here. The staff seems to carry more of a sense of urgency with them. This makes me a little nervous, I haven't had to be a 'real' nurse in a long time. The realization that this new position appears to resemble actual manual labor is shamefully terrifying.

What was also both shameful and terrifying is the fact that I was now officially an orientee again. One of the lowest forms of life in a hospital, right after parking lot attendants and med students. I was already born with a diminished ability to take shit with a smile, and the tolerance I did have, had been rapidly diminishing since birth. The initial hiring phase where I was mainly dealing with the smiling, salesman like faces from the human resources department was over. I would now be left in the questionably capable hands of some crusty old World

War II era nurse who's favorite pastimes likely include rectal exams and crushing the souls of new nurses.

The good news in this new situation, is that unlike on a psych unit, the stereotypical 'sexy nurse' is a lot more abundant here. Maybe not quite at the Halloween costume level….but surprisingly close. An attractive nurse is a unique and especially dangerous creature. All women of course pose a potentially significant threat to the heart, mind, and possibly some bodily appendages to those who pursue them. Nurses not only tend to possess a superior knowledge of human anatomy, they also frequently serve as the inspiration for many male fantasy scenarios. There are probably some bizarre Freudian theories for the latter, but I just assume there is no real logic behind male perversion.

The nursing profession is still largely dominated by females, (who have their own perversions) and tend to fit a certain mold. Although the general population tends to think of nurses as a caring, nurturing breed….in reality, most have developed a distinctive self serving detachment to living world. The days of the smiling mom/nurse neatly draped in white are long gone. Their modern replacements tend to be darker faction, not only in physical attire, but in their very essence. The level of required education is now vastly more expansive, the technology far more advanced, and an amplified workload that can only be described as soul crushing. The addition of an intricate array of new stress factors never even imagined in the early days of healthcare have changed the profession forever. Insurance companies, lawsuits, and politics have complicated the art of healing the sick to an almost unimaginable degree, and the middle man (or woman) of course, is the nurse.

The new 'sexy nurse' is a new grad, no time to be jaded, bitter, or aged by the profession. Today's newly graduated nurse isn't necessarily a 20 something, many are 30 something's looking for some career stability in a market safe industry. The age can be tricky to decipher, a 20 something that has been working in an emergency room for 3 years may have aged about 13 years.... making her easily confused with the 30 something grad bracket. One thing is for certain, the hospital environment offers a surplus of dating adventure for men so inclined. Back then I seemed to be a bit predisposed to dating drama, surrounded by female nurses was a disaster waiting to happen. A really fun, sexy, disaster.

Most *real* adults recognize the dangers of dating in the work place, any work place….but for whatever reason, be it my hopeless romanticism, or my life-long appreciation of rule breaking, a certain glowing young brunette seemed to turn my head almost immediately. It was only day one of orientation and my mind had already shifted from the perils of healthcare practice to the relentless pursuit of women. What I should have been thinking about was the fact that I had absolutely no idea what was going on around me on this floor, not *what kind of an excuse can I come up with to position myself in front of this person?*

This girl was amazing, don't ask me how I knew that from 25 feet away….but a great deal can be observed when you have spent the last 7 years examining human behavior. Although scrubs can be especially deceptive when it comes to revealing the female figure, her posture and agile gait suggested a certain level of athleticism. Upon closer observation a Gold's Gym membership card could be seen on the keys she was still holding on her way onto the unit. I couldn't help but think to myself, *Please be my gym, please be my gym!* I couldn't quite make out the type of car key, hoping to get a hint of what she drove in case there was a need for a future 'coincidental' encounter in the parking lot. At this point I couldn't help but think, *am I a detective of superhero like proportions....or a creepy stalker*. By the looks of this girl, I probably wouldn't be her first restraining order.

As the letters RN BSN on her nametag started to come into focus, my stalker like awareness was interrupted by the person who I apparently was *suppose* to be looking for.

"David?" She asked, as she peered into my line of sight.

"Oh, hey you must be Sylvia" I responded with such professional enthusiasm I actually surprised *myself.* When what I was thinking was, *Jesus lady can't you see I'm ogling one of your nurses!*

I put forth a charming smile and an absurdly fake enthusiastic energy that I would normally have reserved for a girl I was trying to nail. (Before I was so rudely interrupted) As we exchanged professional pleasantries the staff began to take notice, and I could almost feel the 'new guy' buzz fill the air. My mind began to wander into multiple "Scrubs" style fantasy scenarios in which I was the new star of the hospital. Before the entire unit spontaneously broke into a musical dance number in my mind, I was yanked from my fantasy by the sudden realization that Sylvia was walking me directly toward the nurse I was already semi-stalking.

Please God let this by my preceptor I thought, ignoring the somewhat obvious complications that could arise. Not only would that put her in a position above me (and not in the way I was initially hoping), but it would quickly expose my lack of actual medical knowledge that might come in handy on this floor.

As we closed in, she finally looked up at us with what might possibly be the bluest eyes in existence outside of a Disney movie. They were the kind of eyes that probably got her that expensive new Barbie doll every year growing up, and later, half of someone's marital assets. I would go on to describe the smile she initially gave me, but not only did the stroke it caused me skew my memory of the event, but that kind of writing is reserved for Shakespeare and Hemmingway.

"Hey Jen this is David" Sylvia said, while sort of presenting me with her hands as if she was turning a letter on Wheel of Fortune.

We shook hands as if we were afraid we would break each others hands, and exchanged somewhat tentative "heys".

"I'm going to have him just shadowing you today, I was going to have him with Gloria but that might have to be later in the week" Sylvia said. She said it so cautiously it made me wonder if there was a little more to the story. But before I could muster a seemingly innocent question in an attempt to dig deeper she quickly muttered, "If you have any questions or concerns just let me know" as she hustled off down the hall.

And just like that, she was gone, leaving Jen and I alone to our new found, semi awkward, and most likely temporary partnership.

"So you just transferred from the psych unit?" she asked.

"Yes, but don't worry, I was staff, not a patient" I responded, shocking myself at just how lame that was. I thought to myself, *Holy crap David lets not show here what a tool you are just yet, lets let it be a surprise like it usually is*. It was one of those moments where I wondered if she could actually see me cringing at myself, or if she was to busy doing it herself.

Those moments were abundant in my life, so I decided not to dwell on it, I was sure to get another chance to analyze a similarly embarrassing moment, probably before the end of the day.

She shrugged off my attempt at being charming and witty with such raw efficiency I was almost offended. However, since I was neither charming nor witty with that little verbal burp, my work was now clearly cut out for me. I'm not sure what I liked more, her seemingly impenetrable 'coolness', or the thought that maybe she just had a boyfriend to which she was so remarkably devoted to, that even trivial workplace flirtation was not an option. I had heard rumors of such devotion in my boyhood, but personal experience as an adult made such thoughts go the way of Santa Claus and Unicorns. But nevertheless, we all still want that Unicorn under the Christmas tree.

I followed her around the hospital all morning, nimbly redirecting all of the hospital related conversation to something personal. It was a delicate mix of reverse interview questions, coupled with interrogation tactics that would startle the CIA.

During the brief moments when I was actually paying attention to something medical, I was astonished to realize that perhaps I had not forgotten as much technical knowledge as previously feared. Despite my seemingly deliberate attempts to drown nursing school in a bottle of Vodka, with each look at heart monitor or a problematic IV site my inner nerd seemed to climb a little bit farther out of that bottle. While watching Jen replace an IV and some blood plasma tubing I thought, *Holy shit, I remember this….and technically she's doing that wrong.* I snickered to myself. Which was gratifying for many reasons, but mostly because I had anticipated being scoffed *at* on this floor, and now a rush of technical information was ripping its way through my mental rolodex of otherwise useless information.

Its funny how the mind works (or doesn't) I had always been fascinated by it. At this moment I could remember the specific gravity range for urine and the implications of any deviation from it, but would still probably not remember this girls name by the end of the shift, or where I parked my car.

One thing was for sure, despite my best efforts not to be properly 'oriented', it was all coming back to me, and it was all thanks to what's her name. My little side project wasn't going very well and time was running short. I wasn't sure if I would be placed with her again or if this 'Gloria' person would demystify just in time to foil my plot.

As distressing images of what a nurse named Gloria must look like haunted my brain, a familiar and anxiety inspiring sound echoed from the corridor. Although there are many things that beep or ring periodically on a unit like this, certain "alarms" came with a distinguishable sense of urgency that could not be ignored, this was one of them. I couldn't remember exactly what that specific sound indicated at the moment, but an alarm of any kind in a hospital is usually a bad thing, and Jens reaction only intensified that thought.

Her eyes widened as she froze, but only for a brief moment. In hindsight her lack of hesitation and clarity was actually impressive. She let out a little "Oh.." and cut her self off as she dashed to the door. "That's a…" she was cut off again, this time by the overhead PA system.

"Code blue, room 315, code blue, room 315" A calm but firm female voice announced from overhead.

With that announcement she actually broke into a little run down the hall, which caught me off guard, dropping her pen as she scurried into what I could only assume was room 315. She disregarded me much like the pen, leaving me to wonder exactly what I should be doing. I had managed to stay just a few paces behind her during her surprisingly girly run down the hall with only a brisk walk. My genuine concern didn't mix well with my desire to maintain a cool appearance. I was torn between trying to jump in and be a hero, or hiding and pretending I was taking a dump or something they announced the code. Since I was with Jen, the second option was out.

I paused in front of the room as 3 more people rushed in. The room was chaotic and almost surreal as a cardiac monitor sounded so loudly it made it difficult to hear everything that was going on. Nurses shoved tables and chairs out of the way as the infamous 'Crash Cart' rolled in. A nurse feverishly thrust her braced palms into the chest of a thin, seemingly lifeless male patient.

"What can I do?" I asked, hoping the answer was "go help Jen try on underwear".

"Can you jump on compressions?" A young female doctor asked. In the midst of all the chaos and the newly forming knot in my stomach I couldn't help but notice she was kind of cute in a stressed out librarian sort of way. Since saying no was not really an option, I shot in there like I had done this a thousand times.

A *real* code, and real CPR is nothing like television or movies would have you believe. Its not a sexy doctor dramatically pounding his fist against a patients chest and yelling "Live Goddam it!" while a monotone flatline sounds from a monitor in the background and nurses somehow weep and swoon simultaneously. A *real* code is actually far worse; it is a violent, cold a cruel scene. Chest compressions have to be deep, hard and fast. All sex jokes aside, it is a physically demanding action usually resulting in broken ribs and internal organ damage. Large bore IV access is a necessity for the massive doses of epinephrine, lidocaine, and other potentially toxic medications that ironically if they weren't capable of restarting a heart, they would surely stop it.

Successful resuscitation is not commonplace. What typically happens is a temporary restoration of vital signs that last hours, maybe days at best. In elderly or seriously ill patients, we often wonder if it is worth causing all the physical trauma a code entails. But if a person can be saved, and wants to be saved, who are we to decide their fate?

Before I had time to reasonably doubt myself, I was doing compressions. By this time the patient was already intubated, and with each thrust of my compressions I could hear an unsettling gurgling sound being forced out of his mouth. It sounded half human and half mechanical because of the plastic tubing. That sound is forever burned into my memory.

Another little gem that they don't tell you about in nursing school is that compressions are exhausting. As an avid gym goer, egomaniac and lifelong martial artist I could only assume I was probably in better shape than anyone else in the hospital, but after what seemed like only a minute or two at the time, my arms and shoulders were on fire. I felt like I was doing a 'super-set' of bench presses at the gym with no spotter, the whole time trying to appear nonchalant, at least about the rapidly increasing fatigue. As much as I wanted to preserve any shred of coolness, how nonchalant can you really look during a code?

During all the chaos I somehow managed to notice something lightly brushing against my right hip, what made it even more distracting was that my clothing felt a little wet around the same spot. Once that settled in, I had no choice but to dare peek away from my task, if only for a fraction of a second. Nothing good is ever wet in a hospital.

I looked down only to see the patients lifeless, and now bloody arm brushing against my thigh. Another nurse was trying to put in an IV, and excuse the pun, but she was making a "bloody" mess of it. In her defense the patient's veins were likely collapsed due to his current state of virtual death. But apparently not collapsed to the point of not bleeding down my leg. Not only was it not working, but I was now distracted by the needle in her hand about an inch from my leg, and blood that wasn't mine all over the place. *Isn't this how nurses get hepatitis?* I thought. The doctor jumped in to try and get a large bore line into the femoral vein in his hip, but time was running out.

Because the likelihood of this patient surviving the ordeal was slim, and the likelihood of him ever recovering or leaving this hospital outside of a bag was even less likely. A nurse was sent out to contact the family immediately and try to get a D.N.R. order in place so we could end this atrocity.

The infamous D.N.R. order, or "Do Not Resuscitate" is a tangled web of questionable laws and regulations designed to superficially preserve a persons last wishes. Unfortunately there is a lot more to it than that from a healthcare practitioners vantage point. Not only are there many more specific does and don'ts for resuscitation that complicate the plan, but the interpretation of the order can get 'foggy' in the real world of patient care.

Another moral complication developing was the unspoken battle between the 'hospitalist' MD responding to the code, and the ICU doctor that we would immediately transfer this patient to if we were able to get the patients heart beating again. The problem was now, where is this patient going to die? Not *if*. It was either going to be here on this floor right now, or in the ICU, at best, a few days from now. And no doctor wants a patient dying on their floor, under his or her watch, and screwing up his or her MD mortality rate.

So an unspoken war ensues between the doctor running the code, and the ICU doctor. The ICU doctor is pushing for a D.N.R. order so we can let the patient die where he is, and the hospitalist is trying to get him the hell off her floor before he dies right here. Caught in the middle of all this are the nurses, just trying to keep both doctors happy, and the patient alive. Somewhere along the way they forget about that last part. The patient, their families and lives hanging in the balance. A life, somehow the definition changes when it gets wrapped in policies, and it's not you, or someone you love. Somehow a life gets lost in the shuffle.

Finally, after what seemed like an eternity, we are told to stop, record the time, it was over. The nurse had reached the family, and put them in contact with the ICU doctor. Following a brief, and probably very once sided conversation, an official D.N.R. was obtained. ICU doctor 1, hospitalist 0, patient, deceased.

I backed away slowly and put any thoughts of my burning shoulders, Jen, and even my new 'cool guy' status out of my mind. I couldn't help but think to myself, *did that just happen? God, if you're up there....Please take care of this man....* This was the closest thing to a prayer I could muster without feeling weird. I had no sooner finished that thought as Jen reappeared, she had apparently been documenting the code. (There is a detailed form that is typically filled out as the code progresses. It is unofficially the most important aspect of the event to the hospital, the form tends to see the inside of a courtroom more than any other.)

"Hey, they need us outside" she said completely unflustered.

I followed her out, sneaking one last peek at the patient and wondering why no one else did. The nurse's aids were now coming in to begin the post mortem care. This basically consists of one last bed bath in case the family would like to see them before they are 'bagged and tagged' and taken to the hospital morgue. "They're running a little behind now and need us to pick up an admission" she said, dropping off the code form at the nurses station. "It will be a good chance to show you the admit process" she added with a flawless professional demeanor.

I just nodded, "ok" I said, trying to look un-phased and wondering if she noticed the blood all over my leg. I couldn't help but wonder if I was the only one thinking *wait, just wait....I need a minute*. But perhaps the lesson of the day is that there is no minute. A chance to process what just happened was not an option, if we didn't find a way to just shake it off, other patients would suffer and could face the same fate because we were not focused on the task at hand.

I followed Jen into the cramped office behind the nurses' station where we were greeted by an exhausted looking ER nurse and a stack of paperwork. "This is him" she said with a sigh, handing the papers to Jen as if they weighed 80 pounds. "67 year old male, congestive heart failure, hyperlipidemia, came in with chest pain....you know the routine...." she said, so monotone and uncaring she sounded robotic.

"Ok, we've got it....now go home before you collapse" said Jen, flashing a tired version of her patented smile.

We spent the remaining hours of our shift reviewing standard admission protocol and documentation. It was as dry as it sounds, which made my efforts to quiet my mind of the preceding events that much more difficult. I just couldn't seem to shake it off like everyone else on the floor seemed to, did they have something I didn't?

Catching a glimpse through the office door of the body being wheeled away on a stretcher didn't help. I couldn't help but wonder what route they were taking to the morgue. For some reason I pictured them taking the body right through the waiting room of the ER, possibly making eye contact with an awaiting patient, winking at them and saying, "next?"

My perverse little fantasy seemed to humor me just enough to regain some focus. It may have just been some bizarre Freudian defense mechanism to keep me from cracking up or crying, but it had worked. I was back, at least for the time being, and it was time to redeploy some charm. The shift was almost over and I had no idea if I would be working with Jen again in the near future. If being single had taught me anything it was to be opportunistic.

I looked at the clock, and made sure she noticed. "Well" I said, "This has been interesting" letting my exhaustion show through. "So….where's the nearest bar?" I said, as if to sound half joking, hoping she would bite.

"There's actually a little dive bar we go to sometimes right around the corner." She said with unexpected interest.

As the reality of possibly getting a drink with this girl settled in, I found myself thinking, *going to a bar is actually the last thing I feel like doing right now*. But instead, what came out of my mouth was "Do you want to grab a drink and process our stress extremely inappropriately?"

"I can't tonight." She said with a laugh, throwing me a flirty little smile for the first time. I was unapologetically relieved, not only did I *not* have to go out and keep performing, but, I could chalk up that flirty little smile as a small victory.

A small victory, a win, but is that what happened here today? The drying blood stain on my leg said otherwise. Someone died. Someone's entire life, his hopes, dreams, future plans….all gone. I watched man's ultimate fear unfold before my eyes. Was he aware of what was happening? Was he afraid? Was he in pain? So many questions occupying my mind that the regular staff didn't seem to be troubled with. But could I really be any different, after all I still found myself internally gloating about my successful interaction with Jen. Was I actually thinking about death and sex at the same time? As I pondered all of this internal and external drama swirling around my head a truly horrifying thought came to mind....While working in psych, *had I somehow grown a conscience?*

I knew going into this that I was probably in over my head medically speaking. But those fears turned out to be unfounded. What I hadn't prepared for was a deeper problem. Did I really want to stare death in the face on a daily basis? There were definitely some faces I didn't mind staring at around here.... but a balancing act like that couldn't possibly be sustainable or healthy....even for me! What was worse, was this kind of self-exploration was something I was going to have to partake in on a regular basis? If this floor meant doing the right thing 12 hours a day, or even worse, *growing up*, then this might not be the adventure I had signed up for.

Chapter 3

"To succeed in life, you need two things; ignorance and confidence."

-Mark Twain

I awoke the next morning to the soul crushing sound of my alarm clock somehow set on 'buzzer mode'. I would literally rather wake up to *any* other sound, rap music, country music, hell a smoke alarm would pull me out of dreamland with more sympathy than that buzzer. It sounds like I've already given the wrong answer to a question on Jeopardy and it wasn't even 7am. It immediately reminds you of any horrible decisions you may have made the night before, and that you better get moving, the results of those decisions await.

The drive home the night before was a blur. Getting back into my car, the familiarity of the old McDonalds food smell coming from under the seat, and a half eaten candy bar, temporarily brought me out of hospital mode and into my life. But the day's events seemed to penetrate back into my thoughts. How separate can our personal lives and our work lives really be? My mind wandered back and forth from the code blue, to the way Jens hair fell over her iridescent blue eyes. I couldn't help but wonder what such contradictory interests said about the way my mind worked. I fell asleep quickly that night, skipping the usual TV routine, even my incessant web surfing habit took a back seat to my mental exhaustion.

I always had a love hate relationship with mornings. The buzzer of course induced pure hatred, but if I was awake early on my own accord, there was something charming about it. While the drive to the hospital remained the same, my pre-work angst was altered. I had no idea if I would be working with Jen again, or if the mythical 'Gloria' would rear her ugly head. (for some reason I was assuming it was ugly) But the question of the day of course, in the back of my mind, was *would there be another code*. Either way it didn't matter now, I had no choice but to pull it together, it was show time again. Time to be the charming, intelligent, and of course handsome new nurse on the medical floor, the person everyone expected to show up, (at least in my mind) and the person I expected.

I walked through the door of the nursing office coffee in hand, only to be immediately confronted by an invisible wall of anger emanating from an older, disgruntled looking nurse who looked like she may have missed her last few weight watchers meetings. *Hi Gloria*, I was thinking.

This was one of those times when I hated being right. I could only assume she had just received the official word that she would have an orientee today. Lucky me. This woman wore her anger like an extravagant suit. The old descriptive saying, "you could cut the tension in the room with a knife" couldn't be more appropriate. I decided to just sit back, drink my coffee, and wait for the inevitable awkward introduction.

Sylvia slipped on that forged professional smile waiving me over, "Hey David this is Gloria" she said. *Fucking of course it is* I thought to myself, but somehow filtered that into a polite, professional "Hello" accompanied by a firm handshake, eye contact, and the most appealing smile I could gather at the time. *Screw it, let's do this* I thought.

"Hello, I've heard a lot of good things about you" I said, the whole time fighting the urge to make it as sarcastic out loud as it was in my head.

"Likewise" she said, almost certainly fighting the same urge.

"I'm going to let you guys have the north side today, good luck, let me know if there's anything I can do, or that you need" Sylvia said, making her trademark hurried exit. *Yeah, you can get this grumpy antique tank the hell away from me* I yelled in my head. It's always a little shocking just how close those things get to actually coming out of my mouth. On more than one occasion, with the addition of my good friend alcohol, they have.

"Ok, well lets head out to the unit so we can talk" Gloria said with a bit less tension, accepting the situation despite her obvious objection.

"Sure" I said, thinking *this ought to be good*. As she gathered up some papers (and herself) we made our way over to a quiet corner of the nurses station where she sat down, pulled a second chair for me a little closer, and took a deep breath.

"Well as you know I'm Gloria, and I have to apologize, I was promised no more new staff training this year, and this was sort of sprung on me" she said, with the palatable wall of anger crumbling a bit. *Wow* maybe this wouldn't be as bad as I thought? For a second I even thought that maybe I could explain to her that I wasn't technically a 'new' nurse, her apprehension would be lessened even further. I was almost about to feel bad for thinking of her as an 'antique tank' she interrupted with "Now here's how I run things sport". (she actually called me "sport")

While my mind overflowed with sport related fat jokes she continued her self-satisfying little rant. "I was a Navy nurse for 35 years" she boasted, "and I know what needs to get done".

I wanted to interject with something like, *what were the requirements to be a nurse back then? Did you have to know George Washington personally, or just know which hole to put a rectal thermometer in. It was the Navy so I assume pirates were also an issue.* She went on and on with her daily regiment, everything from her morning medication pass to how properly tie my shoes. There was only one way to do anything, that was her way, anything else was wrong and worthy of a court martial. When she took her shift notes from the previous covering nurse, she had a specific pattern she used to write on the paper, new admission information in the upper right hand corner, vital signs on the left. She would stare at me to make sure I was doing it the exact same way. As compliant as I wanted to be, not wanting to make any waves so soon, I could barely fight back the urge to just draw little stick figure nurses being thrown off Navy ships all over the paper while they were giving shift report.

Given this woman's personality I had absolutely no doubt she would turn me in for anything even remotely inappropriate. As we walked the unit talking I felt the need to ask her questions like "Who would I report this to?" or "Who gets a copies of this document?" Deliberately seeking answers that had to do with the Nursing Manager or Director of Nursing, just to reminder that she was neither, and had no actual authority over me. She knew exactly what I was doing.

"So I heard you came from psych" she said, with what I could only assume was her version of a grin. "I've got a couple of patients you might be interested in".

"Super" I said with so much sarcasm I cringed a little bit.

"The guy in 306 has been giving us trouble; he's

definitely psychotic and has been combative with staff" she said. *Awesome* I thought, keeping my sarcasm on the inside this time.

"Well let's have a look" I said, not realizing we were already standing right in front of his room.

Gloria walked in ahead of me of course, I doubted there would ever be as situation she was willing to take a back seat for. I was fine with this because if there really were an actively psychotic patient in there she would be the first one hit with a flying chair. Instead, we walked in on a shockingly thin, feeble looking old man asleep in his bed. Without a word, she started poking and prodding a wound dressing on his right arm. He woke up obviously startled and immediately pulled his arm away. He was visibly terrified and started squirming as best he could toward the head of the bed away from Gloria (kind of like I wanted to all day). His physical ability to move was clearly impaired, and had not said a word yet, making me wonder if he was even able to.

"Here we go again!" Gloria announced with exasperation. "Mr. Murphy calm down!" She bellowed. *Wow* I thought. Who would have guessed Gloria's people skills were not quite adequate for mental health? Sadly, I'm sure she had no idea just how inappropriate and ineffective her drill sergeant approach was in this situation. There were so many things wrong here I didn't know where to start.

"May I" I asked, offering to step in, not to help Gloria, but out of mercy for this obviously mismanaged patient.

"Be my guest" she said, throwing her hands up and backing away as if she had been at this for hours.

I approached the bed, but stopped just short of arms reach, careful not to invade his personal bubble. "Hi Mr. Murphy, I'm David, do you mind if I take a look at your arm?" I asked in the most non-threatening tone I could generate, attempting to re-set the entire nature of his encounter with us. I was afraid the chance had passed because of Gloria's mindless lack of tact. He just stared at me for a moment, maintaining his look of bewilderment. I smiled and just pointed at his arm to nonverbally restate my question. He didn't speak, but slowly and cautiously moved his arm toward me. I advanced with equal caution, more for his sake than my own. I gently removed his dressing and assessed the wound, "does this hurt" I asked.

A very faint "no" came from under his breath. I redressed the wound, quietly talking to him the entire time, explaining each step in simple language I was now sure he understood. Although he did not respond verbally again, it I felt as if he appreciated my method.

I turned around to see Gloria's eyebrows raised as if to

express some sort of disbelief. There were also now two more staff members standing in the doorway, looking at me as if I had just performed some sort of magic trick. "Wow, you've got the touch" one of them said, smiling as she walked away.

"Huh….must be because you're a guy" Gloria said, wasting no time taking a verbal dump on the situation. She charged past me toward the patient, who was now calm despite her rabid Rhinoceros like presence, grabbed the curtain, and rudely pulled it shut. For some reason hospital staff often seem to think those curtains around the bed that provide the illusion of privacy are also soundproof, Gloria was no exception. "It's time to send this one to the Looney bin" she muttered, and stomped her way out of the room.

As it turns out, our so-called Looney Mr. Murphy had absolutely no psychiatric history. He was just an 86 year old man born and raised on a farm in southern Vermont. It wasn't until his late 50's that he was forced to venture out of the comfort of his simple rural existence for reasons that were not his own. After the last of his three boys had left home, this one to college, the previous two had entered the service (like their father) Mr. Murphy's wife fell ill. She had developed lung cancer, and by the time it was discovered it had metastasized to her brain and liver. Like many, she was given an "expiration date", her doctor told them six months at the most. Much like myself, Mr. Murphy believed that humans did not have expiration dates and sought out to find the best medical care possible, unfortunately that meant leaving the comfort of their farm for a place near a world renowned facility in New York City.

Mrs. Murphy received innovative new treatments in collaboration with nutritionist's, therapists, and even meditative healing, all of which were completely foreign to her, but when faced with death sometimes people are willing to push their boundaries. After a couple of months, they found themselves tired, in financial ruin, but....cancer free. Their desperate gamble had paid off. Although they had to sell off the family farm, the oldest son had a place back in Vermont for them to come home to, for them, they had received a miracle.

With the Murphy's new life taking shape, they packed up their few belongings and began their trip back home. It was along route 93 that the city, cancer, and worry, all seemed to be in the rear view mirror, when a semi veered into their lane. In a quick, violent flash their car was on its side sliding to a stop in the median of the highway. The squealing tires sounded like screaming, interrupted only by the thundering sounds of impact that could be felt in Mr. Murphy's chest. As the car stopped and the gruesome sounds subsided, he managed to pull himself from a daze and look to the passenger seat to see if his wife was ok. He froze in horror, not breathing, or caring if he ever took a breath again. His wife's body lay lifeless, while most of her remained in the seat, her head had gone through the passenger window, and was all but gone. Time seemed to stop as he just stared, not realizing that he had been holding her hand the entire time, he pulled himself over to her and just held on.

Paramedics reported having to literally pry him away from her body. The Murphy's had their lives given back to them, only to be taken away. For him, all was truly lost. It was said that he never really spoke much after the accident, to anyone, he just seemed to drift away. As his years advanced and his story faded away, his silence became perceived as senility. He was eventually placed in a long-term care facility where he began to develop respiratory problems, which eventually would land him here, with Gloria and her "Looney bin" label.

My little victory over Gloria felt good compared to the one I had declared with Jen the night before. This one wasn't accompanied by the guild of a patient's death looming over it. David 1, Gloria 0, but I had a feeling this would only add fuel to her fire. It seemed she was the kind of person who found her version of contentment by taking it from others, and I wasn't that content to begin with.

I walked back to the nurses' station hoping to avoid her and have a quick early lunch. An actual lunch break is pretty uncommon in the nursing world, but one of the few benefits of being an orientee, the earlier or later you make your attempt at eating, the better luck you'll have. I managed to find a quiet little corner of the back office with no trace of Gloria. As I began to inhale a stolen hospital sandwich Jen walked in, nearly causing me to choke on it. *Yay*! Almost came flying out of my mouth, luckily it was blocked by a sandwich in my windpipe. As I took a drink of water and gathered myself, she gave that smile I apparently had missed because it actually gave me butterflies. This was getting ridiculous, I hadn't had that sensation since my high school English teacher bent over and inadvertently displayed her 'tramp stamp' in class.

"So I hear you have a gift?" she said sitting down with a bagel, apparently also trying to sneak in an early lunch.

Oh I do, and would love to show you sometime I thought. But I just laughed and said, "What do you mean?"

"I heard you did some sort of Jedi mind trick on Mr. Murphy." I just shook my head. As much as I wanted to claim, yes, in fact I am indeed a Jedi, I couldn't help but feel a little disenchanted. Those in the psychiatric field often claim that 'medical people' have no ability to interact, treat, or even recognize a mental illness....and I was starting to agree.

"This is not the patient you seek" I said, waiving my hand in front of her face. She laughed. I figured the least I could do was lure her in a little more before revealing my true sarcastic and condescending nature. "My Jedi mind trick was actually just taking an additional ten seconds to introduce myself, and *ask* the patient if I could see his wound....instead of just barging in and grabbing him" I said. Her eyes got big as she pulled her head back and looked at me with confusion. *Oops* I thought. That might have been a bit much. "Sorry, occasionally my mouth outruns my brain" I said, in an attempt to bring back that laugh.

"No....you're right" she said, looking at her bagel instead of me. "But its hard, you know how it gets....and nobody cares that you have eight other patients to get to…." She said, almost looking ashamed.

"Oh I know" I interjected, "I'm just saying that when you have a difficult patient, sometimes its all in the approach. Slowing down, taking an extra few seconds can help set the tone for a patient that is scared or confused….I mean….put yourself in their place, before labeling them as crazy…."

She just looked at me for a moment, and then gave me the biggest smile yet, as if I had just serenaded her with a song. Evidently I was able to reel her back in with the sensitive male nurse routine, while hopefully enlightening her a little bit in the process. I couldn't help but feel that our conversation had some genuine significance for her on a personal level. One thing was for sure, I had taken our work relationship to a more personal level, and attaining Jen was looking more and more like a reality.

"I'm glad we have someone from Psych" she said, her eyes now choosing me instead of the bagel. "So how do you like working with Gloria?" she asked. I rolled my eyes, and tossed the remains of my sandwich into the garbage.

"On that note….I think I feel the ground shaking, you better hide your food while I go find her…." I said with a smirk. She covered her mouth trying to hold in her laughter. I quickly made my way out the door before screwing up quite possibly the most perfect interaction I could have had with her. I looked back through the door as it closed, and caught her doing the same, still giggling.

That could not have gone better I thought to myself as I made my way back out to the unit to look for Gloria. I made her laugh, humbled her a little while putting myself up on a pedestal in the process, then somehow made her laugh again. I was in no hurry now to find Gloria and put an end to my good mood. As a wandered around the unit she was strangely scarce, I couldn't help but hope she had went home with her tail between her legs for the day, but that seemed unlikely. After a halfhearted search I noticed Sylvia at the nurses station, "Hey Sylvia, have you seen Gloria in your travels?" I asked, trying to pull myself out of flirt mode.

"Oh yes, I was just looking for you actually….Gloria went home for the day, I guess she wasn't feeling well which is not like her" she said.

"Huh, she didn't even mention it to me" I said, overplaying my surprise.

"Yeah, I was just going to have you review some charts for the rest of the day….or maybe even sneak out a little bit early if you want." She whispered playfully.

My initial thought was that this was an outstanding

turn of events. But the more I thought about it, the more bothersome it became. Either she really was not feeling well, in which case it was still a little weird that she didn't at least tell me she was leaving whether she hated me or not....or worse, she was actually so disturbed by ability to easily handle her so called psychotic patient that she stormed out of the hospital. For me, that would indicate some serious budding mental health problems on her part....Now *who's* the psycho? I thought.

I contemplated milking the clock for a bit while looking through charts, pretending to be diligent for Sylvia's sake. My real motivation of course was another opportunity to try and woo Jen. Eventually logic won out over ego, practically a first for me at the time, and I decided to call it a day.

I made a pit stop through the cafeteria on my way out of the hospital, apparently trying to be cool while I was eating earlier somehow diminished the caloric value of my food and I needed to eat again already. At least that was my self-humoring excuse. Unfortunately this made leaving the hospital through the main lobby afterward my most efficient route. I always hated the main entrance….it was an unfiltered reminder of where I actually was. I could almost feel the people's anxiety as they entered, along with the guilty pleasure of leaving. Generally just visitors use this entry. Staff tend to take advantage of several discrete entry and exit points located throughout the hospital, while most of the patients come in through the Emergency Department. The main lobby made me feel like I was on stage…. only the audiences emotions were very real, from every tear to every ovation, (but mostly the tears) there was no escaping its authenticity.

    I kept my head down and avoided eye contact….The

biggest risk to a clean get away was someone seeing my nametag and asking me for directions, in which case I would uncomfortably squirm while looking at the information desk. And if that didn't work the standard "No habla English" would probably suffice.

I managed to make my way out unscathed, another day another ulcer. The dream of a 'normal job' was starting to look absurd, but my extracurricular activities chasing Jen and symbolically jousting with Gloria probably were not helping. Who was I kidding, I could never joust with Gloria, what horse could hold her up anyway? But not to worry, in the words of Helen Keller, "Life is either a daring adventure, or nothing at all." And who was I to joust with Helen Keller?

Chapter 4

"By night, an atheist half believes in God."

-Edward Young

A key part of any respectable orientation process includes gaining familiarity with *every* shift, although my duties were assigned to the daylight hours, a sample of the 'graveyard shift' was inevitable. I was given an extra day off in between to say goodbye to the land of the living and attempt to prepare my body and mind for pulling an all-nighter. For some, this is their natural state, they are apparently born with a reverse circadian rhythm and a hatred of day dwellers. Much like the psych unit, the midnight shift was a great hiding place for those trying to fly under the radar of administration. This was by no means my first night shift, I had dealt with their kind before…. truthfully, I was looking forward to a Gloria free night.

If you work during the daylight hours, and you ask someone who works at night what it's like….They will tell you that it is torture beyond your comprehension. They will compare it to a sweatshop, describing crushing workloads and treacherous conditions, the likes of which you have never seen. So *stay away* in other words….whatever you do don't come see for yourself. (Because they would have a lot of explaining to do when you woke them up from their nap) Some people have worked the night shift so long they actually believe their own hype, but it's the only shift where you will see people come in to work with their personal laptop bags and a book, which speaks for itself. Things do happen on the night shift, but in general, there is 'down time' that you will never see working during the day, but don't tell them that. In that down time they have the luxury of being able to sort through the charts and point out any little thing that was done wrong during the day, and can make your life a living hell.

When things *do* go wrong at night, they tend to go very wrong. The fact that there is a minimal administrative presence is a double-edged sword. Yes, there is no one to interrupt your Facebook time, but there is also no one to make the big decisions, if something happens and you have to make a tough call….it better be the right one because its all on you.

Ordinary events that might otherwise be considered routine during the day can produce a hectic scene during the night shift if the stars align. (or misalign, depending on your point of view) There are about half as many staff on duty at night, so an increased number of admissions, or even just a patient that does sleep for whatever reason can make the shift seem chaotic. I assumed my first, and hopefully only, night shift on this unit should be a peaceful one in theory. Since I was still orienting, I would not be counted as regular staff, on paper I didn't exist yet from a scheduling point of view, so I would be an 'extra' on the unit. Because I was not hired to work at night, there was no one assigned to officially 'orient' me so I would likely be hanging out with whoever was the charge nurse that shift (or whoever they decided to delegate that duty to). I was somewhat eager to see whether I would be shown the *real* night shift, or if they would put on a show for me to go back and tell all the other 'day dwellers' about.

Coming in to the 'change of shift' report I dealt with the customary new staff greetings, everything from "How are you liking it so far?" to "We haven't scared you off yet?" the usual co-worker banter. I always detested phony conversations that were purely out of social obligation. Maybe that's one of the reasons I was so comfortable around mental health patients, they didn't have those. If a 'crazy person' asks you if they have "scared you off yet", it's not an attempt to appear witty or make amusing polite conversation, they *really* want to know if they have scared you off yet. In general people who are mentally ill, or in an emotional crisis have no time for 'small talk', and for some reason, neither did I.

Children are the exact same way. If a toddler randomly walks up to you and says "you're fat"....guess what....you're fat. They were in no way trying to insult you, or strike up a conversation with an ulterior motive....They just wanted you to know. This is the finest form of communication *ever* in my opinion. Unfortunately the 'sane' adult world has no tolerance for such blunted honesty. It doesn't seem to be a good career choice, and has proven even less successful when trying to court the opposite sex.

We all like to say that we prefer such honesty to sugar coated lies, but we don't. We like to be on the delivery end when making an honest statement, not the receiving end. So in our ever so sophisticated society when someone asks, "We haven't scared you off yet have we?" I reply, "Oh no, everyone has been great", with a smile instead of *"no, but that fat bitch Gloria probably belongs in a straightjacket"*. But that might not be the best way to start off my night.

I made the expected gracious conversation that our society demands during the change of shift. It was a little disappointing just starting my shift, as Jen and the others made their way out with a noticeable sigh of relief, the anticipation of re-entering the real world and their private lives beaming from their faces. But for the night, I was one of the 'vampires' working the graveyard shift. Part of me really wanted to come in with a pillow because I thought it would be hilarious, but I doubted my particular brand of humor would go over very well this early in the game.

The ruler of the night shift was evidently a guy named Richard Deets, a former Army medic turned Nurse who looked a little too much like 'Mr. Bean' for me to take him seriously. Despite his appearance I was relatively certain my pillow joke would not have been appreciated. Either way I was stuck with him for the night. There was always a sense of awkwardness when two male Nurses work together, we always look at each other and think, *I wonder why this guy became a Nurse*. Each presuming there was an underlying reason for their career choice in a female dominated profession.

The unofficial 'right hand man' for 'Mr. Bean' was an elderly African American woman named Martha who looked meaner than rabid boar. She was surprisingly soft spoken for a boar, with a slight southern accent designed to make you let your guard down while she plotted your death. She rarely initiated a conversation, but when speaking with her, despite the soft southern drawl, it seemed every smiling word contained a stifled *fuck you*. She was the quiet worker bee of the night shift, people left her alone and that's exactly how she liked it.

But I would be spending my night with Deets, in my mind, referring to him by his actual last name was probably better than Richard or Mr. Bean….it lessened the risk of accidently calling him 'dick' or making a Mr. Bean reference out loud. As a former military man, he was probably used to being called by his last name. As for Martha….well, I just planned on avoiding her and I was sure she was planning a similar course of action.

Deets began talking with me as if we were old friends already in the middle of a conversation. "So they finally made the guy in 301 a DNR today", I just nodded in acknowledgement as Martha gave a slight eye-roll and a sigh of relief. I even heard Jen mumble, "It's about time" under her breath as she walked out of the room.

The rest of us followed her out on to the unit, poised to begin our shift. I heard another voice behind me mutter, "Nice….from slow code to no code" with a muffled little chuckle. I wasn't really sure what that meant, so I turned around to see who it came from, but just caught a glimpse of Martha and the back of another nurses head.

I had never heard the term 'slow code' before and thought maybe I had misheard whoever said it. The cynic in me began to envision some sort of developmentally delayed patient in room 301 and staff that was seemingly even less politically correct than me. I decided that could not be the case, however I must have heard her correctly. Besides, anything other than the word 'slow' would have ruined her little rhyme, 'slow code to no code'. I had to know what it meant....and since Deets and I were apparently old friends I blurted out, "what's a slow code?" making no attempt to hide the genuinely puzzled look on my face.

He quickly recoiled as if he wanted to put his hand over my mouth, "Shht", he stopped himself from rudely 'shushing me' or swearing, I wasn't sure which and I don't think he was either. Then he let out a little laugh, "hold on sport" (*SPORT again, really, what the fuck*) "I'll explain that in a minute, just let me get these to Sylvia before she leaves." He held up a hand full of shift reports from the night before and trotted off to catch up with Sylvia at the end of the hall, his 'trot' was a little something less than one might expect from a former military man. *Oh come on Mr. Bean, now I REALLY have to know* I thought to myself, now in psychological anguish over this mystery hospital phrase. The suspense was killing me, for some reason I was afraid it might come up in conversation with someone in the next five minutes and I still wouldn't know what it meant. I pictured it being a deal breaking lack of knowledge with Jen, and her riding off into the sunset with Deets. (Trotting no less)

I found a nice semi-visible location at the Nurses Station and sat waiting with my best 'I'm ready for my big talk' look on my face. I probably looked like I was waiting to hear about the 'birds and the bee's' for the first time from my Dad. My eyes followed his every movement as he made his way back toward me, I made sure he noticed, to ensure he made no attempt to escape. He smiled and pulled up a chair, "So you came from psych eh?"

"That's right" *Don't change the subject* I internally squealed.

"I'm guessing you didn't see a lot of codes over there" He said. I just shook my head no, trying not to delay the conversation any further.

"Over here….well on any medical unit really….we get a lot of geriatric patients, 80s, 90s, the guy in 301 is 86. The point I'm trying to make is that they are on their way out, one way or another, whether they know it or not….sometimes it's the family that doesn't know it, or won't accept it. So when, *not if*, they code (referring to a 'code blue' specifically, cardiac or respiratory arrest) if they don't have a DNR in place, we are expected to go charging in guns blazing the same way we would if they were 12. We all know they are not going to make it, and if they do get a heartbeat back, they're not really back, if you pump enough epinephrine into a rock you will get a heartbeat….A person that age typically doesn't wake back up….and even if they do, they now have 7 broken ribs and are covered in bruises….and for what….to live another day and a half? In pain?"

I didn't think he was looking for an actual answer from me, and if he was, I didn't have one to give him. So I just waited, allowing him to continue.

"So, what unofficially happens is this…. When that code comes, instead of going charging in, we purposely take our time….We walk to it…. we go through the motions so to speak. We technically do everything we would normally do, just not quickly….allowing the patient time to die. Peacefully, instead of in a bloody blaze of glory. Do you know what I mean? This is what they are talking about when you hear the term 'slow code'....but don't let the wrong PR people, or management ever hear you say that. Management knows, most of them used to work the floor so they know the drill, but obviously it's not real PC. You can see the potential controversy right? On paper, everything looks the same, the family is satisfied, and the 'we did everything we could' routine is laid out for them. The patient was going out anyway, we just save everyone from more grief....including us."

"Ah...." I said quickly, trying not to appear dumbfounded without much success. "I see what it means now at least....That is indeed a touchy subject." I added, being entirely caught off guard by the profound implications and depth of such a practice. If I had known what it was something so grim and disturbing I probably wouldn't have asked. In truth....I didn't know what to think. My initial reaction was that it was wrong, totally and utterly wrong, but the Nurse in me wanted to argue. *Was it?* I wondered. Well it depends who you ask I guess....

One thing I did know for sure was that it wasn't legal by any stretch of the imagination. But like he said, on paper everything looks legit. When push comes to shove, or at least a courtroom, what is documented is really all that matters. A code blue was run, every step of it, just very slowly, which would be almost impossible to prove.

But would running a full code on someone like the patients he described just be delaying the inevitable like he said? According to everything I was ever taught during my formal education, he was technically right, the chances of them surviving a code were slim to none, and the chances of making a full recovery were next to nothing. But 'next to nothing' is *not* nothing…. If there is even a fraction of a chance someone could be saved, his or her life fully restored, isn't it our job to at least try? Who were we to be playing God?

I didn't have a lot of time to ponder this gem of an addition to my hospital jargon repertoire. The infamous night shift was upon me, and the longer I sat and thought the more danger my 'cool new guy' reputation could be in. I put my indifference mask back on and allowed Deets to change the subject to something more mundane. I couldn't help but be a little surprised by the amount of trust he had just bestowed on me, he didn't know me at all. One would think that kind of information would be kept under tighter wraps, he had essentially just ratted out the entire hospital for illegal euthanasia. Manslaughter was another term that came to mind, along with malpractice and murder, it was starting to sound like a demented nursery rhyme in my head. *Manslaughter, malpractice, and murder oh my* to the tune of The Wizard of Oz song stuck in my head. (Lions and tigers and bears, oh my)

Before my mind completely broke into a show tune, the sound of another one of this units imposing alarms made its way down the corridor. This one didn't sound quite as menacing as the one leading up to a code, but it warranted our attention, so Deets and I made our way out of the station to see if we could track it down.

As we got closer to the source we could hear the sound of a male voice raised in what sounded like a heated argument, which was actually *not* typical on a medical unit. As I instinctively started to pick up the pace, I noticed Deets just rolling his eyes and shaking his head. "Someone you know?" I asked.

"Yeah, it sounds like Becky needs rescuing, the guy in

302 is a nut job….maybe *you* should take this one." He said giving me a little nudge with is elbow like we were 12 and he was daring me to go talk to a girl.

Nearing the door of room 302 we could now distinctly hear the argument taking place. "This is bullshit….I'm done with this fucking thing, the doc said it would be 2 days!" the male voice roared.

"Mr. Hanson please don't yell, the IV is going to beep like that when the bag is empty." A quivering female voice responded.

"Then get here before the fucking thing goes off!"

"Mr. Hanson…." She paused, almost anticipating an interruption.

"Go get someone who actually knows what the hell they're doing!"

Before we could get to the center of the action a young Nurses Aide came storming out, chased by the crashing sound of an IV pole hitting the floor. Her face was red, eyes watering but refusing to cry. "I can not deal with him anymore....I just f...." She stopped herself, still clinching her teeth.

"Relax Beck" Deets said, putting his hand on her shoulder.

"He's fucking crazy and I just want to go home" She replied in a whisper, pulling herself together. She looked at me and apologized with a soft "sorry", shrugging her shoulders, showing a little embarrassment.

"No need to be" I replied.

Before I could offer any comfort or change the direction of the conversation to something more comfortable, Deets interjected, "In all seriousness would you mind going in to do his meds a little later....you might be a little better suited for him."

"Not a problem" I said with a smile, as if I knew how

to handle him. They acted as if they were sending in a hostage negotiator. I was just hoping to get a look at his chart so I had a clue what was going on with him before they sent me in blind. It seemed they were expecting another 'Jedi mind trick' from the Psych Nurse. *I'm not the crazy person whisperer* I thought. I could already see myself getting pigeon holed as the 'go to' guy for this sort of thing, a bouncer for the medical unit.

The three of us headed back to the Nurses Station and I made a beeline for the charts, if I was going to impress again I needed this guys apparent psych history. I grabbed the only chart marked with the last name 'Hanson' and dove in. He was in for an infection that he had acquired shortly after surgery to repair a herniated disk in his back. Nosocomial infections are increasingly common. (Infections acquired while hospitalized) In recent years it has become such an enormous issue that most insurance companies refuse to pay for treatment, forcing the hospitals to either pay up, or prevent them. Since he had been discharged after the surgery, then readmitted for this infection, the hospital would probably foo t the bill, but not before a lengthy battle with the insurance company and of course passing off whatever cost they could to the patient.

There was absolutely nothing mentioning a psychiatric problem in his history according to his chart, although I did notice that the man's first name was 'Leslie', maybe he was still mad about that? Not finding a persons psychiatric diagnosis isn't entirely uncommon when they are hospitalized strictly for a medical concern. A shrewd method for a medical professional to find an uncharted diagnosis was to examine his medication list, an antipsychotic or even antianxiety medication would be a huge red flag. But again, I found nothing, not even an antidepressant or a sleep aid. *Oh well*, I thought. This wouldn't be the first time I had to deal with a patient without having any real information about them, nor would it be the last. I couldn't help but feel a little uneasy about going in to start his IV medication that was coming due, not only was I going in blind, but I was going in with something that he was already unmistakably furious about.

I gathered as many IV supplies as I could, so that I wouldn't need something while I was in there, then have to leave and go get it. Not only would this make me look like I didn't know 'what the hell I was doing' which I already knew he liked to point out, but it would be adding another visit which would probably be accompanied by another altercation of some kind. Like a good boy scout, always be prepared. Knowledge of his most recent battle with hospital staff was the best information I had to go on at the time, so I wasn't entirely unarmed.

As I made my way down the hall to his room I passed Becky in the hall who gave me a sarcastic thumps up as she whispered "Good luck". I jokingly gave her a little growl, then politely knocked on his already open door. I stood in the doorway and saw a well groomed middle aged man with short greying hair sitting up watching TV and looking miserable. Not miserable in the sense that he wasn't physically feeling well, but miserable in the sense that he was just waiting for another opportunity to bark at someone. I was not about to give him that opportunity.

"Mr. Hanson?" I asked, cautiously entering the room, but letting him notice my size and maleness at the same time.

"Yeah" he muttered, his eyes widened a bit as he pulled his head back. "You're a big fella….They send you in here to straighten me out?"

I just smiled, "Straighten you out?" I asked. He started to shake his head and before he was about to speak I talked over him, "I can straighten out this IV pole that seems to have had an accident....Your doctor wants us to get this antibiotic in you so I need to set this back up." He lowered his head submissively.

"Yeah....I'm sorry about that"

"Don't worry about it" I said, now that I had set the tone of being in charge, I wanted to lighten it up and see if I could keep it friendly.

"I haven't been able to sleep since I got here with that thing constantly beeping, I thought I was finally done with all this after the surgery, and then boom, right back here again with an infection that I supposedly got from staying in *this* hospital."

"I know, that sucks, but try and take it easy on the girls ok, they're just doing their job." I said, still keeping the conversation light and building on our rapport.

"I'm an asshole when I'm stressed out and tired….I will try and go easy….but its hard being in this friggen place." He said, without a trace of the aggression I had overheard earlier. He even modified the 'f' word, presumably for my benefit. I had purposely used the word 'sucks' earlier in an attempt to let his guard down and make a connection. My tactic had either worked, or I had made him uneasy, I considered either one a conquest in my favor. My initial impression was that he was right, he was an asshole, a bully to be more specific. Like most bullies, it was easier for him to take out his anger and aggression on females, or anyone he perceived as weak enough to just take the abuse without reprisal.

"It can be very stressful being in a hospital, but hopefully we will have you back home soon" I said, trying to wrap up our passive aggressive little discussion.

I finished setting up his IV in silence. I left his IV pole with a few dents and scratches in it from his earlier fit in his room as a reminder of potential danger for any staff that enter, as well as an antagonistic reminder for him to keep his cool. As I walked out the door I asked. "Is there anything you need before I go?" just so no one could say I was anything but polite and professional.

He mumbled, "Yeah, get me out of here" under his breath, then said out loud "No….I'm all set". I pretended I didn't hear the first part, and walked away.

Walking down the hall I could see several staff gathered around the Nursing Station now looking at me with anticipation. They must have been congregated there the entire time waiting to catch flying debris, or at least listen in on my little adventure. Becky looked at me with a smile, she threw her hands out to her sides and let out a "Well?" a little too loudly. Deets just stood in the background shaking his head, I assumed at her.

I threw my hands out mocking her for my own amusement, "what" I asked as I arrived.

"Well what happened? I didn't hear any yelling, did you smother him with a pillow or something?" she asked, part of her probably wishing I had.

"Asphyxiation would be a bit of a red flag on the autopsy silly girl…. I pushed him out the window, duh…." I said, pulling a 'Deets' and talking to her as if we'd been working together for years. Everyone laughed, even Mr. Bean himself let out a little chuckle. It was a calculated risk on my part letting my unvarnished sense of humor fly so early, but it seemed to land well.

"Come on, seriously, how'd it go…. what happened when you went in with another IV?" Becky asked smirking.

"First of all let me clarify something for everyone, he's

not crazy.... he's just an asshole.... There's a difference...." I said with a little fear of coming across as arrogant, but hoped we were now all aligned with my particular brand of humor.

"Oh, he's a psycho" she said.

"He's not actually, I assure you, he's a calculated asshole with bully like traits" I said, mimicking how an actual mental health diagnosis out of the DSM might sound. (Diagnostic and Statistical manual) "Seriously, he is absolutely *not* crazy....a jerk, yes....but as far as I know that is still not treatable condition."

"Oh its treatable....It's treatable with a smack up side of his head." She said.

"I'm not sure how we would bill for that....Hey Deets, what is the billing code for bitch slap therapy anyway?" I said, pushing the envelope a bit.

"I'll have to check with Sylvia on that one" he said, I

took his mention of a superior as a hint that maybe it was time to tone it down, although Becky was laughing hysterically and even Martha was fighting back a grin. Either way I decided it was time to conclude my little performance.

"Ok, time to chart my trivial adventure with Mr. Hanson. But seriously, he really doesn't have a mental health diagnosis….sometimes a difficult patient is just a difficult patient." I said, sincerely trying to broaden their minds when it came to my weird area of expertise. I wanted them to understand that anyone under the right kind of stress can act out, it is not reserved for the criminally insane as some people would like to believe. I went into the back office and took as much time as I could to thoroughly chart my interaction with him. Difficult patients tend to be the first ones to sue, usually they go unfounded, but this particular patient already had reasonable cause to complain with his hospital-acquired infection. There was bound to already be an internal investigation underway, and unlike most of my documentation, someone might actually read this.

Methodical charting was also a great way to kill some time, activity on the unit was dying down and I didn't tolerate boredom well. My collection of paper airplanes and paperclip men would surely be impressive by the end of the night. Maybe not so much 'impressive' as it is disturbing that a nurse in a hospital has nothing better to do with their time at work. After finding no further 'I's' to dot or 'T's' to metaphorically cross I decided to take a walk around the unit and see if anyone was up to anything interesting, a little sightseeing on the night shift so to speak. I wandered down the hall and eventually ran into Martha talking to a couple of other staff I hadn't seen before. It had the appearance of a relaxed conversation, but there was an edge to it I couldn't quite place. As I got closer Martha made very deliberate eye contact as if she had something to tell me, it appeared that walking past this creepy little conversation was no longer an option, so much for sightseeing.

"This is Stacy, she's a case manager, and Reverend Peirce." Martha said as she opened up their quiet conversation circle for 'the new guy'.

"Hi, I'm David" I introduced myself by name because Martha had not, I assumed she had forgotten my name, this was a trick I had used myself many times during awkward moments such as this. I smiled at Martha as I spoke, I wanted her to know I knew what she was doing.

"Mr. Johnson in 301 just passed" Martha said.

"Oh" Was all that came out of my mouth for some reason. I guess it is human instinct to apologize and offer condolences when someone announces a passing, but what do you do in a hospital with a co-worker? "Is there anything you need me to do?" I added. What I wanted to say was *wow that was quick.* This was the patient they had just made a DNR for on the previous shift, and just like that he dies? How courteous of him to abide by our schedule. As an array of insanely inappropriate thoughts continued to fill my mind I was glad they were not actually coming out of my mouth for once.

"No no I just wanted to let you know, we're taking care of everything" Martha said in her hushed southern style, almost shoeing me away now. As I prepared to make my departure I couldn't help but notice the social worker looked like she wanted to tell me something. Martha notices as well and interjected , "Actually, could you just run in and grab his monitor, they were looking for one on 4 East earlier."

"Sure" I said, reversing my direction and going into

301 as if it was in no way uncomfortable. The three of them headed to the office while I fumbled for the light switch. I could see from the light coming in from the hall that his body was covered with a sheet, which made me feel a little bit better about finding the light switch. The room had an eerie calm, everything was clean and in its place, nothing like what would have been found following a code. It was peaceful.

I grabbed the monitor she had asked for, and noticed a fully charged IV pump right next to it, I presumed that would also now be useful someplace else. The pump still had a half filled bag of Potassium Chloride hooked up to it that the patient was being treated with, as I unhooked the bag and various tubing I couldn't help but notice the date on the bag, it was dated for the previous day. That was strange because another bag should have been started today, long before he passed away. Either it had been mislabeled, which was unlikely because whichever nurse had dated it probably dated hundreds of other items during his or her shift, if anyone knows what day it is, it's a nurse. The other explanation was that the next bag was never started. I turned the IV pump on to see if there was any indication of how long it had ran, but it had already been reset.

  I was immediately brought back to my conversation with Deets, and wondered just what kind of other liberties hospital staff took with other peoples lives. *Could someone have really just stopped all of his medication the second the DNR order went through*? If so, was it an honest misinterpretation of what a DNR order encompasses, or a deliberate act with a very specific end result in mind? As disturbing as the latter was, it would not be the first time I had heard of such an issue. During my clinical training as a student, I once had an instructor stress the fact that a DNR order only means 'do no resuscitate' it does not mean 'do not *treat*'. The fact that he felt the need to stress this to a group of students indicated that the two were confused often enough that he needed to add it to his curriculum.

While to most people this all probably seems like 'common sense', a legitimate debate has transpired within the medical profession as to what developing conditions should be treated when a patient is not expected to survive, but modern DNR orders tend to be very specific, and are not the same as Hospice care criteria. Hospice tends to lean toward 'comfort measures only' when dealing with a patient. Their idea is to let the patient pass away with as little pain or discomfort as possible. A DNR order has nothing to do with that, and is not reserved for patients under Hospice care. The man in 301 was *not* under Hospice care.

I took one look back at the covered body as I walked out the door, almost dropping the monitor in the process. I wondered if maybe I was just letting my imagination run away with me, the stress of a new position, or lack of sleep. This couldn't be what it looked like. I considered finding a way to indirectly ask Deets about it, but decided against it. I had probably caused enough trouble with my little rant earlier, perhaps accusing one of his staff of murder wasn't the best way to end my night.

The best way to end my night was evidently a combination of cyber stalking my new co-workers and wandering aimlessly around the unit trying to stay awake. Most of the staff didn't even attempt to keep themselves alert until about 20 minutes before the first of the day shift crew began to arrive. Appearance was everything for them, the most important thing was to just be out of the office and on the floor in case someone from administration arrived early. I just hid in the back drinking coffee, I had no intention of sleeping when I got home anyway.

Next to the coffee machine was a colossal bulletin board cluttered with mandatory hospital information mixed in with employee yard sale ads and band flyers. My overtired mind found some sort of symbolism between the cluttered board and the hospital itself. Something about the chaos mixed with order, important information side by side with something meaningless.

As I read about an upcoming seminar on eating disorders and considered having ice cream for breakfast I heard someone approach. I was in no mental state to engage in any kind of conversation so I just moved out of their way, pretending to be completely enthralled in what I was reading, never taking my eyes off the bulletin board. After they passed by behind me, I couldn't help but peek and see if it was someone from administration. I looked….and looked….but there was no one anywhere near me.

A chill went up my spine as my mind desperately tried to rationalize. It wasn't that I necessarily *didn't* believe in ghosts, but I was to tired for anything else, I was unquestionably exhausted, and clearly not thinking straight, but if anyplace was going to be haunted it's a hospital. "Wow, on that note….goodnight Mr. Johnson" I actually said out loud, hoping no one could hear, and decided to call it a night. I wouldn't be volunteering for any overtime on the graveyard shift.

I stayed up the entire day following my seedy night shift experience in order to properly 'flip' my sleep cycle, a method most shift workers are familiar with. But there was another reason for my sleep avoidance that my growing delirium was feeding into nicely, and that was an unabashed fear of the inevitable nightmares stemming from my recent experiences. The past couple of days alone had included everything from traumatic codes and medical murder to ghosts. I was probably a matter of hours from developing a full-blown case of hypnophobia (Fear of sleep).

After I had done everything I could think of to stay awake, including getting kicked out of the gym for spilling coffee on a treadmill, I figured it was time to face my irrational fears, (One of them at least) and go to sleep. It had been about 36 hours and my brain was starting to melt, although according to recent studies the human brain can go about 96 hours without sleep before *significant* brain damage occurs. Not being 100% sure of the extent of the damage years of alcohol and combat sports had already caused, or what exactly they meant by 'significant' brain damage, I decided to play it safe, and stay well inside of that 96 hour mark.

Chapter 5

"The insane, on occasion, are not without their charms."

-Kurt Vonnegut Jr.

I awoke after what seemed like about 2 minutes of sleep with the sun beaming in perfectly with laser like precision between uneven blinds directly into my eyes, an inch in either direction and I could have been spared. As a dream about brain damaging ghosts slowly faded from my memory I decided it was time to face a new day, it was back to the day shift and according to the schedule I was paired up with Jen again.

There was something about the morning that made it easy to shake off my hospital murder theories, and even dismiss the ghost. It was a Friday and my status with Jen was optimal. What was it about sex that over powered every other concern in the mind of a male? In my mind, getting what I wanted from Jen would somehow cancel out everything else. Logically I understood that this was one of those situations where getting exactly what I wanted would probably leave me with even more problems, complicating my already complicated existence at the hospital.

The complete egomaniac in me just wanted the satisfaction of knowing that I could have her if I wanted, but the weak minded buffoon in me would surely follow through if given the opportunity. Who was I kidding, I had no intention of straying from my well established self destructive pattern of behavior, I was living the dream, a profession surrounded by woman….crazy, damaged, women. And I was frequently the damaging mind mangler that helped them on their way.

I pulled into the staff parking lot early enough to find a spot that wouldn't require a GPS signal to find my car again, this was a first for me. I let the song 'More Than a Feelin' finish playing on the radio before jumping out of my car coffee in hand, right into the face of pure evil, Gloria, I had parked *right* next to Gloria! *Son of a bitch* I thought, but it came out "Oh hi" instead. She looked up at me just as baffled to see me as I was her, no doubt thinking *son of a bitch*, or whatever the ancient demonic equivalent was in her native language.

"Hello" she said, not even making eye contact before she went drudging off ahead of me. At least I pretended to have a pleasant demeanor, she wasn't even trying. I let her walk off ahead of me while I took a second to check out what a woman like that drove. I expected a 1960's style hearse, or at least something pulled by several horses, but it was actually worse because it was so mundane and unassuming. No one would ever guess that a late 80's model tan Pontiac was the main source of transportation for such evil, but the fact that it apparently had the power to haul elephants was quite impressive.

It was too late to dive back into my car, or even pretend I had forgotten something, this incredibly awkward walk to the hospital was going to happen. I made every effort to stay just far enough behind her that I didn't need to try and engage her in conversation, but just close enough to not be weird. I even ran up at the last second to open the door for her like the gentleman I wasn't. She mumbled a quick "Thanks", I just smiled and thought, *see how nice I am?* I couldn't help but wonder if turning into Gloria was the inevitable future for the nurses I damaged along the way, was there a 1942 version of me that made Gloria the way she was? Probably, but I had come way to far, and put way to much effort into this little project to grow a conscience now.

I made my way through the various unpleasant smells of the hospital until I reached a pleasant one, coffee in the back office. It was especially busy this morning, bustling with Nurses and various hospital staff either trying to get out of there, or trying to settle in for the day. That many people heading in the opposite direction in such a confined space was only endurable with coffee. I had always loved the smell of coffee, but not so much the taste.

I had only recently begun to 'need' it for survival, there was something about the medical unit that made me feel like I might need a little extra kick in my blood stream. This was probably a very dangerous path to start down, statistically Nurses have the highest substance abuse rate among any other profession, specifically prescription drug abuse (probably because it is so easily attainable for a Nurse), and maybe coffee was my gateway drug. I could see it all unfolding now, a coffee on one day, a rectum full of stolen narcotics the next, all just to deal with the occasional hospital patient murder they would probably just blame on the drug addicted nurse anyway.

Just in time to save me from my self-induced anxiety attack that evidently only stolen narcotics could alleviate, in walked Jen. She almost bounced in like Tigger from Winnie the Pooh, it would have been really annoying that early in the morning if she wasn't so ridiculously cute. She had a ghastly looking green health shake in her hand, apparently opting out of my new coffee program that ultimately leads to narcotics in your anus. Of course I had no sooner finished that thought when I found myself looking directly at it, her marvelous, presumably drug free ass, right in the office in front of at least eight coworkers. This was hardly the first time I was guilty of that, however this *was* the first time I had an audience, which unfortunately included Jen.

While the others thankfully decided to pretend they didn't notice, Jen did not. She looked me right in the eye, cocked her head to the side and said "Good morning David" with the kind of smile a mother gives her child when she catches him in the cookie jar.

An overly enthusiastic "Hi" shot out of my mouth before I had a chance to think of a witty cover. I was at least mindful enough not to shout out "*no no wait, I was just thinking about shoving narcotics in there!*" It had been my experience that someone drinking a green health shake instead of a coffee in the morning might be just the kind of person to take something like that the wrong way. I was in desperate need of a temporary distraction, what I wouldn't have given to have the cool-aid man come crashing through the wall. Luckily the next best thing boldly interrupted my fumbling attempt to recover the situation, Gloria. She literally walked directly in between us even though we were only about 2 feet away from each other, I was surprised she fit.

"I think you're with me today" Gloria said with surprising poise considering her hatred for me. "I've got some more crazies for ya" she added.

As my heart sank into my shoes, Jen intervened. "Actually Sylvia had him on the schedule with me today" she had an unexpected cattiness in her tone that caught me off guard, I almost expected a little head roll or a finger snap to accompany it. Mental images of a Jerry Springer style 'cat fight' temporarily distracted me from the loathsome idea of spending another day with Gloria. As much as the man in me wanted to see two girls fighting over me, the fact that one of them was a psychotic rhino sort of ruined the experience.

"Oh, with you? Really?" Gloria returning Jen's tone. The underlying intent being a jab at Jen's age and experience level compared to her own.

"That's what it says" Jen's voice lifting as she presented us with a copy of the schedule. She didn't have to convince me, but apparently Gloria was looking really forward to another shot at me, even having some more patients to verbally and psychologically abuse in my presence.

"Ok" Gloria said with audible disbelief. As she walked away and headed straight to Sylvia's office, not about to have her plan foiled so quickly. I exaggeratedly mouthed the words "thank you" to Jen, much to the amusement of the remaining staff in the office.

"You're welcome!" she yelled loud enough to be heard from the next floor. I laughed out loud, completely taken back by her complete disregard for professionalism or respect toward Gloria….it was official, I was in love. I couldn't help but think, *what the hell was in that green shake?*

"Lets go, we really might have a crazy one coming up from the emergency room today" she said, as we walked out of the office I had to take a moment to gather my thoughts and make sure I wasn't the one now bouncing around like Tigger from Winnie The Pooh.

We listened to a nurse from the previous shift give us the details from the night before and the potential warnings or 'adventures' as I liked to call them, that may lay ahead for us. The person coming up from the ED didn't have much of a diagnosis, dehydration and two of my all time favorite bullshit diagnosis's 'failure to thrive' and 'psychosis NOS'. (NOS simply means 'not otherwise specified') In other words, the doctor probably had no idea what was wrong with this person. An elderly dehydrated person could easily be showing signs of confusion or disorientation, and failing to thrive….well that just means they aren't doing so hot. It's a shame we can't have a private version of hospital documentation that simply tells it like it is.

The nursing aids had already brought her up to a room and were getting her situated. I could hear pleasant sounding conversation coming from the room as we approached, but as two of the aids left, one of them was laughing so hard she had to literally cover her mouth with her hands. They just looked as us as they walked out of the room giggling like little schoolgirls. Needless to say my curiosity was peaked. Jen just looked at me as if to say 'that was weird' and slowed down so that I could walk in first. Apparently she was more hesitant to enter a room where people were laughing than some of the others I had seen her go running into where alarms were blaring and bodily fluids were flying, this, for some reason, gave her pause.

I walked in room 308 to find the lovely Mrs. Veronica Enslow sitting up in her bed, alert, oriented, and has hydrated as could be. Her bright smile nearly lit up the entire room as she looked at me and said "Oh good, the beetle-frog is here with my surfboard…."

"Ahh…." I said, now trying to stifle my own laughter and looked over at Jen who was just frozen, eyes as wide open as her mouth. "Well hello Mrs. Enslow...." I paused, debating whether or not to through in something hilarious, yet highly inappropriate for my own amusement. "I'm sorry….is this your surfboard?" I said, pointing at Jen. (I guess there wasn't that much hesitation) Jen remained frozen but somehow I felt my joke was appreciated.

"It's right there!" She said, pointing at my pen. This

was getting good so I decided to just let her run with it, eventually Jen would either snap out of it and jump in, or pass out. I had a plan for either scenario. She leaned forward and I let her take my pen from my hand, something I wouldn't normally do with a psychiatric patient.

"This….this got three of my children pregnant…." she said while staring passionately at the pen. She was looking at it like they were old lovers with a secret past, everyone's comfort level was rapidly diminishing, I decided to intervene before she went in for a kiss.

"Mrs.Enslow….Mrs.Enslow….do you by any chance take any medications?" I said, reaching out cautiously for my pen, my child molesting, rapist, pen.

"Oh, wait….the pentagon…." she said, as if she had just remembered the answer to a question someone asked her a year ago. She stared at me intently as if I was supposed to have an immediate response from the same universe she was in. I capitalized on the brief distraction and retrieved my pen before she could do anything crazy with it, or before it took advantage of her. I caught a glimpse of Jen who was no longer frozen, but seemed to be thawing out to a wonderful shad of red from fighting back her laughter, at least one of us was trying to maintain a sense of professionalism.

"Is *THAT* where I know you from Mrs.Enslow....the pentagon?" I said, immediately regretting it, realizing I may have crossed a line with that one. It apparently wasn't an entire waste, it made Jen do a literal 'about face' and scoot out of the room, I heard her burst into laughter the second she made it into the hallway.

"The pentagon is where it all happens…. pens…. lightning bugs…. the whole lamb and scooter…." she said, staring off into the distance, reminiscing it seemed.

If she was gazing off into another world we now officially had one too many realities intermingling in this room.

"Well.... On that note, Mrs.Enslow I'm going to see if any tests are in.... I'll be back to check on you, the lighting bug situation.... and the whole lamb and scooter...." I said, walking out of the room before I caught myself having a little too much fun with poor Mrs.Enslow.

"Don't forget your pen" Jen said as I met her in the hallway, now laughing so hard she could barely get the words out, tears rolling down her cheeks. She covered her own mouth trying to regain her composure.

"I think you might be enjoying this just a little too much my dear." I said, doing my best to convert my goofy smile into a sexy smirk. "Did they at least do a UA down stairs?"

"A UA? What, are you afraid she's pregnant or something?" She laughed.

Seriously? I thought, could she really not know about this? Before I could decide how smug I was going to be about this, the words were already coming out of my mouth.

"In the elderly, a urinary tract infection can cause symptoms of mental illness, even psychosis." My words may have been educational, but I had a feeling my face and tone were a little condescending. I wasn't overly concerned, a situation like this went right along perfectly with my current theories on how to woo the opposite sex. Maybe if I showed a little superiority she would be honored if ever given the opportunity to 'please me'. A wise friend would later tell me that my theory held true for girls, but not women.

She pursed her lips together and gave me an adorable

little scowl. "Well, no one leaves the emergency room without a UA, so we'll find out." She said, turned away and headed back toward the nursing station. I couldn't tell if she was pissed off at me, or just pretending to be. In hindsight, she was probably just in hurry to see if I was wrong.

I sped down the hall after her, for what was probably the only legitimate reason in our brief history together. "We should probably put her on a one to one observation don't you think? She's a little too unpredictable for my comfort level." I said, knowing we probably didn't have the staff available for something like that, but I was genuinely concerned she might do something, well…. crazy.

"A one to one? You think she's that dangerous? A tough guy like you afraid of a little old lady?" She said, attempting to return a little playful condensation. I wasn't quite sure how to proceed, I wanted to keep things on a flirting basis with Jen, without getting sued by the family of a patient that jumped out a window or something after an adulterous pen.

"Ha ha, actually I'm just a little concerned that she might be a little *too* detached from reality at the moment. She might try to swan dive into the toilet, or eat from the garbage can or something."

Jen just smiled, but there was something different about it this time. "Well I saw the way she was looking at you and your pen, I would hate for you to be involved in any kind of sexual harassment suit." She said, giving me a little nudge with her shoulder as we walked into the nurses' station.

Wow, I thought. Not only was she initiating physical contact, but I was pretty sure she just brought up sex. "Did you see that outfit?" I said, throwing out my sexiest smile. "She's totally asking for it."

Jen stopped and smacked her palm to her forehead, laughing in disbelief. "Oh, my, God, you did not just fucking say that!" She said, still trying to contain her amusement. I couldn't help but think *wow, the f-bomb, she is totally comfortable around me, and probably in love with me*. How could she not be? I've been pulling out all the stops from day one!

"Speaking of sexual harassment," I said with a malicious grin. "I'm pretty sure today calls for that drink…. I will even leave my pen at home to avoid any temptation."

She brought her eyes to the floor and took a step closer, invading what would have been my personal space if she weren't so gorgeous. I had a brief flash of a fly, flying into a spider web. "I'll tell you what… If it turns out that Mrs.Enslow has a UTI, we'll go have that drink. And if it turns out that its the sole cause of all this, and she's ordinarily completely normal…. I'll buy."

"Deal," I said, and jumped on to one of the computers to see if any results were in. Bad day for Mrs.Enslow, good day for David. *Now…. How do I get into the lab to contaminate that sample…. Just in case?* As I logged on the to the hospitals clinical software, I actually started to contemplate ways it could be done, but I couldn't risk doing anything that might really get me into trouble.

I had no sooner dismissed my deceitful contemplations, when yet another of the hospitals distressing alarms started shrieking its way into the office. Another code no doubt, they hadn't announced it yet, but I recognized that sound. Jen and I shot out of our chairs simultaneously. We entered the corridor and merged with other staff heading in the same direction, nobody was saying a word, which led me to believe this was not an expected code, even some of the more seasoned vets seemed a little surprised.

We were met halfway down the hall by two nurses and a doctor heading in the opposite direction, they were shaking their heads and motioning for us to turn back. We all slowed to a stop, and I noticed that the Doctor wasn't a Doctor, it was Deets. I had made the age-old assumption that the male in the group must have been the doctor, shame on me. I was so puzzled by my own outdated assumption, especially being a male nurse, that I almost overlooked the obvious question. What was Deets doing here at this time of day? It was still about 2 hours before the next shift, yet here he was, responding to a code no less.

A few of my fellow responders just turned back and went about our business, while Jen, myself, and a few others met Deets and the nurses. "Hey David" Deets said, almost preemptively it seemed, before the conversation began.

"What happened? Was that Mrs.Barnett's room?" Jen asked, sounding not only genuinely concerned, but a little bit angry. I had no idea who Mrs.Barnett was, but apparently Jen did.

"It was, she just passed. I'm sorry Jen I know you had her for the past few days." Deets said, putting his hand on her shoulder. I wanted to yell out *get your God damn hands off of her*, but thought that might be a little weird.

"I just didn't think she was going to go so soon. She had just told me *yesterday* that her family was coming in today to discuss some of her affairs." Jen said, as if she was cross-examining him.

"They were in early this morning, while I was still on with Dr.Carter" Deets replied, still talking to her as if he was comforting his teenage daughter, soothing, but stern.

"It was good, they looked like they had a nice visit before heading out, they talked, signed some paperwork…."

"What paperwork?" She asked.

"Just the usual stuff, you know, power of attorney, DNR."

"A DNR…." She took a deep breath and just stared at him.

"Jen…. You knew she was terminal." He said.

The tension was palatable, but brief. She snapped back into nurse mode, a little more hardened this time, just like some of the others I had seen. Is this how it happens? How many times can a person deal with death, before it takes something away from them? Before they grow a suit of armor, not to keep things out, but to keep any more of their soul from escaping.

Jen still had her soul, but between the hospital, and guys like me, it was diffidently in peril. We walked back to the nurses' station in silence. She had seen her share of codes and lost her share of patients, but I could tell this one made a dent in her psyche and I didn't know why.

"Are you ok?" I asked, hoping the answer was yes. My plan to get her out for a drink after work was now clearly in jeopardy. Hopefully somewhere inside of me, in my other 'head' perhaps, my concern was more sincere.

"I'm fine, it just caught me off guard ya know? I had her every day this week except today, and today she goes…. Its just weird." She said. I couldn't help but wonder if she was trying to be tough for my benefit. I was torn, I wanted to lighten the mood, maybe redirect the conversation, but the white elephant in the room was glaring. Was Deets here to oversee another one of his 'slow codes'? Maybe his theory wasn't has universally accepted among hospital staff as he made it sound.

One of his special codes wasn't even necessary with a

DNR in place. Maybe that was when his henchwoman Martha stepped in. *Was Martha on last night, could this really be happening?* I thought. One could definitely argue that a pattern seemed to be emerging, but what did I know, this was a hospital and people die here. If I were to say something, people would probably just assume I spent too much time on the psych unit and was being paranoid. But if I didn't say anything and it was real, what then? What would that say about me?

I dove back on the computer in an attempt to re-create the vibe just before everything happened. I subdued my urge to drill her with questions about codes and hospital deaths only to nourish my urge to just 'drill her' in another sense. It was time to lighten the mood, and I had found just the thing, Mrs.Enslow's urine test had come back positive for a UTI. It was time to mentally switch gears for the greater good. Or so I convinced myself.

"Do you want to know what else is weird?" I said, spinning around in my chair like an evil villain. "Mrs.Enslow has a UTI."

"*Fuck*, seriously?" She laughed. "Shit! Well she probably got it from your perverted pen, who knows where that things has been."

I chuckled, genuinely impressed with her quick wit. "Well, it's a Nurse, and you know how they are." I said.

"That doesn't mean that *that's* why she's crazy. I may not have worked psych, but I'm pretty sure you can just be crazy *and* have a UTI without there having to be any correlation." She playfully argued.

"Very true" I said with a smirk. "But maybe I also took a look at her medical record? A woman that age has been in the hospital a few times and guess what, not *one* admission to the psych unit!"

"Ugh…. Ok so she's never *actually* been admitted,

maybe they just treated her outpatient? Maybe she went to another hospital…."

I interjected before she could finish, "Oh my God stop, it's *just* a drink!" I laughed. "I will even let you off the hook a little and not make you buy. How does your foot taste anyway?"

"Oh *you* stop" she said, teasingly slapping me in the shoulder again. "Its just one drink" she added, making quotation marks in the air with her fingers. "Is probably how a lot of bad decisions get their start."

"God I hope so" shot out of my mouth before I had a chance to stop it. *And why not* I thought, I needed to test the waters a little while I had her back in a more lighthearted mood. I was confident I had a good bead on her now, maybe it was time to push my luck.

She just laughed, "Oh my God you're terrible" she said, shaking her head. "How do I get myself into these things?"

"You don't, you were carefully guided and manipulated every step of the way." I said, outwardly cracking myself up at this point, astonished at my own merciless honesty that was now clearly spiraling out of control.

"Ugh…. Stop talking!" she exclaimed, still laughing. "I said I would go, geeze, learn to quit while you're ahead!"

Ahead I was. Finally, this was going to happen, and it only took a few carefully influenced bonding incidences involving death, disease and human suffering to make it happen. *Totally worth it* I chuckled to myself.

Before a sense of euphoria could completely settle in, the door to the office swung open revealing an appalling site, Gloria. In all the excitement I had almost forgotten she existed. Nonetheless, between the brief onset of bliss, and Gloria's presence, a sense of balance was restored in the universe. Nothing like a cruel reality check to remind me that failure was somehow still an option. Somehow all of the deep philosophical witticisms rushing through my head simply came out as, "Hi Gloria".

"Daaavid...." She crooned, stretching my name, maybe to match her size. Even her words ate too much. "So I was talking to Sylvia earlier, and have I got a little pet project for *you*. Its right up your ally. Come take a walk, I need to steal you away for a minute."

I stood up and shot Jen my best 'help me' look to no avail. I wanted to say something to her like 'stay' or 'sit' to make sure she didn't disappear before I could get back. I had absolutely no doubt Gloria had been planning this curve ball for days, leaving me at a slight disadvantage. The one advantage I did still have, was the knowledge that she was outdated, crazy, and probably couldn't make it up a flight of stairs on her own (just incase I had to outrun her). At least this time she had the foresight to involve Sylvia in her plot, no doubt unwittingly on Sylvia's part, but throwing her name in gave the whole thing some credibility, which was all she was really after.

The fact that she had gone through the trouble of running whatever it was by Sylvia to bypass any intervention by Jen was a bit worrisome. She took her time with this one, not allowing her psychotic impulses to take charge, this was cold and calculated, I may have underestimated her after all.

"So, we were talking about how *great* you are with psychiatric patients." Gloria said in almost a motherly tone. A surprised, sarcastic mother who was just caught off guard by a good report card and didn't quite believe it yet.

"Since there seems to be more and more of them

making their way onto the med unit, and we wanted to see if we could find out why." She added, elevating the sarcasm to an almost accusatory pitch, as if I had brought them all with me from the psych unit or something.

I didn't even attempt to wipe the look of revulsion off of my face as she walked me into a small, semi-abandoned office at the end of the hall. It smelled of failed careers and budget cuts, the only place that wasn't covered in dust was a 90's era computer mouse accompanied by the outline of an ass imprint on the chair. This was probably the hiding place for a nightshift staff looking at porn, or maybe for another job, like I should have been doing.

"So you've noticed an increase in psychiatric patients requiring medical care?" I said in a corrective tone.

"Well yes…. we just wanted to put some real numbers on it, and see if we can get to the root of the problem."

She replied, laying it on thick, trying to pretend she wasn't just trying to assign some extra homework to the new kid.

"So what exactly would *she* like me to do?" I replied, passive aggressively reminding her that my duty delegation fell under Sylvia's title, not hers.

"We were hoping you could dig through the old patient charts and help us put together some kind of report for the budget committee. Something that would reflect our *real* staffing needs verses that of the regular psychiatric unit." She explained.

"Are you looking for more staff? Sitters for one to ones, things like that?" I asked, trying to hide my skepticism.

"Well why should our staff ratio's be the same as theirs, when we have our *real* patients and the nut jobs on top of that to deal with?" She said with the all of the confidence of a deranged southern politician, arguing against desegregation.

Real patients, wow, really? I thought to myself, holding back a verbal outburst that would have surely required my resignation. "I'll see what I can do" was all I replied, but I have no doubt my expression and tone conveyed my true loathing.

"Great, well this room is yours for as long as you need it." She said with a smile that I was sure would reveal fangs.

"Super" I said, eyeing the door, hoping one of us would soon be walking through it.

"I'll leave you to it" she said, wedging herself out the door.

So this was brunt of her attack, on the surface I wasn't impressed. But the underlying message hit its mark. It wasn't so much *me* personally that she had a distaste for, (in fact I bet there were very few things she didn't like the taste of) it was psychological health as a whole, having a legitimate place in her world. The fact that doctors, nurses, and the patients themselves are now much more likely to recognize mental illness, and to pursue its treatment in a traditional setting was something she could never adjust to. It is now being recognized as a *real* problem, and a valid illness that required authentic management, and not just being brushed aside, or even locked away. For whatever reason, this progressive movement seemed to be her nemesis. Maybe it was progress or evolution in general she feared, maybe she thought that if things continued the way they were she might have to take a closer look at herself and who she had become. I refused to believe she was born an angry hippo.

The one thing I couldn't deny was her vast experience,

fact that she was fighting a losing battle could not possibly have eluded her. But like many people experiencing mental anguish, she had to find a way she could exude some form of control, she may not have been able to lock her 'problem patients' away how she wanted to, but she was able to tuck me away in this dusty little office dungeon, at least for the time being. For Gloria, I was a symbol of the enemy.

I plopped myself down into the chair releasing a billow of dust into the air that almost made me choke. The abandoned office was far enough away that it softened the hectic sounds of the unit. Without Gloria, it was peaceful, without Jen I could finally think strait, maybe this grimy little forgotten corner of the hospital was the place for me after all, or maybe just a preview of coming events, my career already gathering dust.

Alone with my thoughts, in isolation, I started to

imagine what it must be like to be a patient here. A patient with a mental illness that was being ignored because a physical one took precedence. I thought about everything I had learned, the purpose of this place, its importance, and my roll in the grand scheme of things. In retrospect, I'm not sure what came over me, but the way I saw it I had two choices, I could sit down and diligently begin to sift through mountains of data in order to produce a dazzling report for the powers that be, humoring Gloria and reinforcing her outdated philosophies in the process. Or, I could give them the report they needed, instead of the one they wanted. I could write up a report that would reflect the gross mishandling of patients with psychiatric needs, overlooked by staff that lacked both knowledge and interpersonal skills.

As tempting as the second choice was, it would be

unfair to condemn the entire staff for their lack of information and experience. Failing to recognize mental illness in a hospital setting is more of a system error, than any individual one. But the real problem ran deeper. The hospital, a place where the sick came to be healed, had developed a sickness of its own. Its culture was sick, the staff was sick, and didn't even know it. The illnesses that were battled everyday within the walls may not have been able to penetrate the staff physically, but the mental and spiritual toll it had taken was clear to me now, more than ever.

The pinnacle of this illness has taken shape with the creation of the 'slow code'. Those that had come into the profession with the desire to heal the sick and fend off death had now become deliberate deliverers of death themselves. I was becoming more and more aware of the possibility of something even worse than *that* was happening right underneath all of our noses, there was something happening on the night shift that was even darker than the bags under their eyes. I just couldn't prove it.

When life gives you only two choices, I always tend to go with the third. Yes, I was stuck in this corpse of an office for the rest of the shift, and probably even longer, but if it was data collection they wanted, that's exactly what I would give them.

My mind was made up. I'm not sure if it was the dust in the room clouding my brain and better judgment, or if Gloria had finally just pushed me over the edge, but I was now determined to take this opportunity to dig into the records for my own little investigation, something that mattered more than adding room in the budget for a few more staff. Perhaps the poor lighting in the room was just right for growing a conscience.

Like the beginning of any great project of mine, the best time to begin was going to have to be tomorrow. After all, I had a date to think about, which made this no time to be growing a conscience.

Chapter 6

"Love doesn't make the world go around, love is what makes the ride worthwhile."

–Franklin P. Jones

My grand and virtuous scheme to expose the misdeeds of the night shift almost over shadowed the sensational victory that had already taken place. Jen and I were indeed going out after work, and although I had played this exact scenario out a thousand times in my mind, I was a little apprehensive. We were about to partake in a major workplace taboo, although she probably didn't see it that way. Despite my ego's best efforts, I could only assume that Jen looked at this as no more than a friendly after work hangout. My objective was obviously a little more dubious, but no more so than any other red-blooded male on the planet.

Although the workplace element of the situation added a bit of complexity, it was far to late to begin thinking logically now. I thought to myself, *maybe I would extend the invitation to Gloria, as a chaperone, surely she could suck the romance out of any situation, or perhaps buy her a few shots of whiskey and challenge her to a race home?*

It was time to focus on the matter at hand, and bury away any lingering bitterness from my most recent encounter with Gloria. The last thing I wanted to do was to turn our hard fought night out into a work meeting gone sour. I was certain Jen already had her own issues with Gloria, and I didn't want to set the tone in that direction. Getting this girl to go out for a drink had already proven to be a monumental task, so this was no time for a rookie mistake.

I found Jen sitting in the break room with her coat on, a light blue, slightly oversized North face coat, looking like she was waiting for a ski lift. She was vigorously texting with the focus of a neurosurgeon. This was either an intense 'text fight' or she was trying to squeeze in a thorough update with a girlfriend about the super hot guy she was about to go out with. I preferred to assume the latter but was not about to take any chances.

"Hey there, are you looking up UTI induced psychosis?" I asked, hoping to interrupter her with a laugh, and remind her exactly why we were going out. Not only because of a playful bet, but because I was irresistibly charming and hilarious. (lets not forget modest)

She smiled, tilting her head to the side and gave a sarcastic little "ha ha" as she turned her phone face down. "I wasn't sure you were ever coming back, do I dare ask what Gloria wanted?" she asked.

"Oh she wanted see how much food she could fit in her

mouth and wanted to see if I would…."

"Oh my God stop" She interrupted, giggling and swatting at my arm as she stood up. "She's probably still here somewhere you dork! I think she prowls the halls after each shift."

"I'm kind of glad you stopped me, I have no idea where I was going with that." I said while pretending to shy away from her adorable little attack. Clearly our relationship had elevated to a level allowing physical contact, and I intended to soon to test its limits. "Speaking of having no idea where I'm going…. where are we going?"

"I was thinking the Pub? Actually I have no idea what its real name is, we just call it the pub. It's a little dive bar right up the street."

"So should I throw on a tie, or rip the sleeves off of my scrubs?"

"Definitely rip the sleeves off your scrubs." She laughed.

"Listen, there will be plenty of time for ripping my clothes off…I mean, slow down, I hardly know you." I said, giving my best fake scowl.

"Ugh" she said, rolling her eyes while somehow maintaining her sexy grin. It was however, probably time to pump the breaks a little with the sexual innuendos, at least until I could get some alcohol on board.

We left the unit together, and even though we had left at the same time before, I felt as if it was obvious we were up to something. It was a paranoid, school age butterfly sensation that I hadn't felt since my brief and uneventful 'marijuana phase'. I'm not sure what exactly I was so paranoid about, but the walk out of the hospital seemed to take an eternity. She led the way out of the building using a lesser-known side door, used primarily by maintenance. My non-marijuana induced paranoia made me wonder if she was also feeling a need to slip away unnoticed.

"So do you want to ride with me? My trunk is surprisingly spacious." I asked, obviously not only failing to slow down the innuendos, but kicking the creepy level up a notch.

"Ha ha, that's ok, there's probably no room next to that dead hooker anyway." She fired back.

"Its fine, she's a midget." I replied without any hesitation.

"Oh my fucking God you are going to be so much trouble." She laughed. "I really don't want to leave my car here, someone might think I really was kidnapped."

We were parked close enough not to lose sight of each other in the parking lot, relieving a little anxiety over any last minute unforeseen snafus that could kill the mood.

She didn't look back at me while getting into her car, which brought it right back. She drove a little black Volkswagen Jetta that seemed to suit her, although I would have expected a happier color. Maybe there was a touch of darkness in her she could only express with her automobile, or maybe I was overthinking the work of a slick car salesman.

I speed-walked to my car while attempting to appear as casual as possible, but the second I was inside the gloves were off. I threw my things in the back had it running and in reverse so fast I nearly ran over our unit secretary backing out. At this point, her death would have been a small price to pay to ensure a smooth trip to 'the pub' with Jen.

My short, but feverish drive across the parking lot was completely unnecessary, as Jen had pulled over to the side to wait for me. I pulled up behind her and we were off. I did my best to use this time to relax, almost a meditative state before the real game would begin. As I struggled to stay directly behind her, I pictured the drive as a sort of metaphor for our relationship to each other. The pursuit of any woman was not unlike this drive, there were periods where it was easy to stay together because there was no outside interference. Then there were the obstacles, poorly timed traffic lights trying to separate us, aggressive drivers trying to wedge themselves between us. Like with any relationship, we had to find a way to communicate when words were not an option, in order to stay together.

    I couldn't help but notice there was no place in my little metaphor that addressed the possible need for one of the cars to quickly drive away immediately after reaching its destination. There was nothing to address the fact that the cars might have to park right next to each other in the same garage every day, whether the pursuit was a success or not. Just as my alpha-male brain tried to take over and reignite my anxiety, we pulled into a little place called 'Half Pints' otherwise known as 'the pub' in Jen's world.

We were able to park right next to each other, which didn't allow much time for any last second primping. I got out of my car first and took a deep breath to try and obtain some clarity. It was unseasonably warm, overcast, but hardly worthy of her little blue ski jacket. Without making it too obvious I was able to glance in her car where it looked like she was frantically texting again.

She hopped out of her car almost as joyfully as she seemed to bounce into the office every morning. I caught her checking herself in the reflection of her driver's side window before walking in my direction. She smiled and looked like she was about to say something when her cell phone lit up.

"Sorry, my roommate keeps texting me, she's having some issues so I invited her out, she loves this place." She said, while typing a somewhat lengthy reply.

Fuck! I thought, fighting hard not to express that thought outwardly. Was she setting up a chaperone of her own? I just smiled, delaying my response for a moment as we made our way to the entrance.

"Great. Women with issues, alcohol, what could possible go wrong?" I said, only partially trying to mask my discontent.

"Hey, plenty of men have *issues* as well." She said, making little quotation marks in the air.

"Yes, but we tend not to show them…. We just bottle everything up inside until it hardens nicely into a mental illness of some kind."

"Oh *that's* healthy" she laughed.

"Speaking of health…. So this is the pub?" I said with

a smirk, opening the door for her.

"Thanks, yes, in all its glory."

We took a pair of seats near the center of an almost empty bar. They were a little tattered, and a shade of green that likely saw its peak in the 1970's. The bar itself was somewhat sticky, not quite like you would find in the basement of a frat house, but a little out of the comfort zone of a nurse trained in microbiology. There was only a hand full of tables that weren't likely used for anything other than a place to drink, on the rare occasion the bar was unavailable. The walls looked like they were white at some point in time, but had collected enough dust and cigarette smoke to take on all the glorious colors of a prison bathroom.

"So what do you drink? I'm not sure you're going to be able to get a green vegie smoothie in here." I said just loudly enough to attract a glare from the bartender, a heavy set woman that looked like she could hurl me out of there like a Frisbee.

"Ha ha, don't worry, I'm a whiskey girl, none of that fruity garbage for me"

"A whiskey girl, wow and I thought this was going to be a low key night, I had no idea I was going to end up having to break up bar fights and clean vomit. I could have stayed at work for that!" I said, while silently thanking God she was a 'whiskey girl'.

"Don't get your hopes up." She laughed, and signaled the bartender.

She ordered a whiskey sour, making me almost hesitate to order the light domestic beer that had become a primary ingredient in my weekend adventures. I was afraid I would hear the usual *"watching your figure sweetheart?"* that I had come to expect from my more virile friends. Not to be outdone so early I boldly added a couple of shots of tequila, taking a bit of a gamble.

"Ooh boy, you really are trouble." She said, not hesitating to reach for her shot.

"You have no idea" I said, making slightly extended eye contact.

She just smiled, lifted her glass and said, "To our new psych nurse".

I smiled and countered with, "To Gloria!" causing her to nearly spit out her shot.

We just sat on our beat up green stools and talked about all of the drama that had taken place since my arrival to the unit. Every high note leading to another shot of tequila, and our need for personal space diminishing. For some reason we stood up to take our shots, and when we sat back down, our bar stools were a little closer together every time. Every joke was a reason to touch me on the leg, or the front of my shoulder as if she was trying to cop a quick feel of my chest. *Isn't that my job?* I thought, at this point I had to take as second and make sure I hadn't said that out loud.

"So, what made you get into psych?" She asked, shifting out of drunken gossip mode for a moment, her leg now permanently resting against mine, instead of the occasional 'accidental' brush.

"Well, insanity runs rampant in my family…. so I guess I really just wanted to know where I came from."

"Come on, I'm serious…. tell me something personal for once!" She said, not looking all that serious with a piece of lime stuck in her teeth.

I knew I had to give her something more than a snarky response, but sharing personal information was definitely not my strong suit. I had a fleeting thought about how nice it might be to just completely open up about my personal life, the mental illness that really did seem to have a genetic tie to my family, or maybe just my sad, painful childhood in general. But that was very dangerous ground, and I had to stick with what I knew best. A hint of something deeper, tied in with a joke, would give her a sense that there was something more to me. That, combined with alcohol, is a powerful weapon against a woman's better judgment.

"Maybe I didn't have the happiest of childhoods, and wanted to see if I could figure out why people do the things they do?" I said, purposely staring off to the side a little bit to let her know I was a little uncomfortable, maybe even vulnerable, if that's what she wanted to see. I waited just long enough to let the prospect that I was hiding something serious sink in.

"Maybe that's why I slept with Gloria?" I added, resuming eye contact and pulling us right back into our jovial form.

"*Oh….my….God….*" She said, laughing hysterically. "Can you imagine? Hell, that's probably exactly what she needs!"

"Ha! What she needs is a padded room, or a straight jacket…. well she might be in to the straight jacket thing, who knows."

"Careful with Gloria…. I might get jealous." She added, touching my side as she stood up.

"Oh?"

"Perhaps, you never know. I'll be right back I have to find the bathroom."

I made sure to show no enthusiasm, I was Mr. Cool as I watched her disappear around the corner. *YES! Holy shit! Thank God for alcohol and my demented genius* I thought to myself, probably doing a little dance in my bar stool. I ordered another round while she was in the bathroom, along with two more shots that I would now refer to as 'deal closers'. I even had time to posture myself in the manliest stance I could muster as she made her way back to the bar.

"Holy crap it was freezing in there!" She said, nestling herself up against me as she picked up her shot.

"In that coat? You could climb mount Everest, in January!" I chuckled, as we took our shots. I opened up my jacket and said, "Here, you can jump in with me."

She put down her empty glass and just stared at me, with what seemed at the time like some form of restrained elation. She was clearly contemplating something in her mind I would probably enjoy.

I picked up her whiskey sour and took a drink. "Wow, you can hardly taste the roofie in there." I said with a completely strait face, knowing she was now well versed in my dry and somewhat deranged sense of humor.

She grabbed my open jacket, pulled herself close, and

kissed me like we were standing at the alter. It was surreal, I could almost hear the 'oohs and ahs' from a sitcom studio audience in the background. From my perspective it was a gigantic relief, as if I had just crossed the finish line of the Boston marathon.

The rest of the night was a bit of a blur. My last, relatively clear memory was of the only rational decision either one of us made for the remainder of evening. At some point we came to the conclusion that neither of us should drive anywhere, and called a cab. I do however recall a lengthy conversation consisting mainly of me explaining to her why walking 4 miles to her apartment at 1 o'clock in the morning, probably wasn't a good idea. She would later refute that story with one of her own, where she evidently had to explain to *me* that taking a *limousine* 4 miles to her apartment was equally, ridiculously, unnecessary.

We obnoxiously stumbled through her apartment door, convinced at the time that we were being quiet and courteous neighbors. I couldn't help but notice how much nicer her apartment was than my own. I expected cleaner, and a coffee table *not* made of pizza boxes, but this place was incredible. It smelled like flowers and spilled day old liquor, which in hindsight may have been coming from me. She dragged me by the hand past a huge kitchen with marble floors and new stainless steel appliances, down a wide hallway with several anonymous doors. We landed in a whirlwind on a large bed that seemed dangerously high off the floor. The rest was a blurry mix of broken buttons and high-risk fluid exchange.

Chapter 7

"Sex is an emotion in motion." –Mae West

I woke up engulfed in a multilevel panic. An abrupt realization that not only was I naked and in a strange place, but I had to either throw up, or shit my pants…. if I could find them. Sadly this was not the first time I had found myself in this situation, but familiarity is not always a skill builder, especially for this particular scenario. I had no idea where the bathroom was, and going exploring in the nude, in an apartment I wasn't sure we were alone in, seemed inadvisable at the time.

I began looking around the room as carefully as possible, barely moving my head, not only because it hurt, but also because I wasn't prepared to deal with a more coherent Jen just yet. The room looked like some sort of bisexual clothing bomb went off. A wide spread trail of clothing, knocked over lamps, and general destruction, although impressive, made it very difficult to spot any clothing I could make a dash for.

As my bodily functions started to truly insist on taking priority over any attempt at modesty, I felt Jen begin to stir. Although I had been laying there in a panic for what seemed like an eternity, I played as if I had just begun to wake as well.

She took a deep breath as she opened her eyes. "Oh my God, I'm such a slut." She groaned, putting her hands over her face.

"Maybe not? It might have just been really warm in here last night, there is very little evidence pointing to the contrary." I laughed.

"All because of a little old lady, with a UTI that apparently makes you crazy." She sighed.

"Oh yeah…. About that."

"*What?*"

"There may be a *slight* chance she was crazy anyway…. I really have no idea what her medical history was." I said with a wary grin.

"You *asshole!*" She yelled, and began beating me with a pillow.

She was trying to be playful, but with every blow I came closer and closer to grabbing the pillow by the case, and throwing up in it. The only stomach settling aspect of the whole thing was the fact that she was still completely naked, which was more distracting than a hangover any day. I assumed the fetal position and attempted to plead my case.

"*Wait wait!*" I laughed. "She really did have a UTI…. I just didn't pull her medical history yet! I swear I was going to!"

"I should have known, you're such a shit."

Speaking of shit I thought to myself, I needed to get to a bathroom as soon as possible, and this little 'morning after' pillow fight is only cute when one of the participants doesn't crap themselves in the process.

"Ok ok, I'm a terrible person, but if you don't point me to your bathroom pretty quick something more terrible is going to happen right here." I said, still trying to hide my anguish.

"I'm pretty sure something terrible already happened here. It's the first door on the left. Maybe…. maybe I'm a big fat liar face too!" She playfully scowled.

I gingerly slid myself out of the bed to ensure minimal exposure for both of us. Luckily my feet landed directly on my boxer shorts, apparently drunk David even had enough foresight not to hurl them across the room. I put them on with the speed of a gunfighter, it looked as if Jen was paying no attention anyway, but I couldn't take any chances, if I were in her place, I would surly only be pretending to be aloof while taking mental photographs. (and probably a few real ones)

I walked with as much poise as I could, for someone probably holding back a diarrhea and vomit extravaganza. A rush of relief filled me as I made it to the bathroom relatively unscathed. I turned on the water full blast for some auditory camouflage and let loose. Fortunately my body let me get away with a quiet, relatively discreet, bulimia style spew and I was back in business, maybe even ready for round 2.

I couldn't leave the bathroom without taking a quick peak around, a woman's bathroom can tell you a lot about her, things she would never willingly disclose. It was a little late, but I took a quick look around her medicine cabinet for any prescription antibiotics, antifungals, anything indicating what I may have contracted the night before. There was nothing strikingly incriminating, not even any signs of recent male visitors, just one creepy one, rummaging through her bathroom.

A momentary booger check in the mirror, and I was headed back to the bedroom, Jen's bedroom, I couldn't help but wonder if this had really happened. An almost overwhelming, and surely undeserving sense of satisfaction and accomplishment washed over me. My smug little Zen moment was short lived as a walked through the door and realized Jen wasn't in there. *What the hell? Did she make a break for it? That's my job!* I thought. Just as horror was about to set back in, she came through the door behind me. She was completely dressed in an oversized hoodie and sweatpants, but carrying two bottles of water that canceled out my disappointment with her lack of nudity. Leave it to a nurse to want to rehydrate.

"Are you going to make it? Need an IV?" She asked, handing me a water bottle.

"A forensic rape kit maybe." I replied, with a cringe at my own tactlessness.

"Ugh, eloquent as always."

I gathered my haphazardly dispersed clothing from around the room and began to reassemble myself as best I could with a female watching over me. Bits and pieces of the night before were starting to come together in my mind. As many things as there might have been to love about this girl, the primal male urge to flee the scene of the crime was starting to become overpowering. The chase was over, and it was time to retreat back to a place where I could contemplate my next move, a 'fortress of solitude', or in my case, something closer to a super-villains layer might be more appropriate.

"Well, I'm in pain. Partially from the booze related

dehydration, and partially from your brutal beating. I should probably go home and regroup." I said, part of me hoping she might protest a little.

"Alright, well, do you want a ride to your car? I'm hoping my roommate is here somewhere and will bring me back to mine."

I had completely forgotten the fact that I was miles from where I left my car, and that there was a slightly mysterious roommate that never showed up the night before. I couldn't help but wonder if there was any truth to that, or if she was just on standby to rescue Jen if things went badly with me.

"No, that's ok, I could use the walk to pump some of the toxins out of my body." As I spoke I was realizing just how far away my car actually was.

"Are you sure? Its kind of far, she should be up soon, if she didn't have a night like ours last night."

"Last night *is* a little fuzzy, she could have been *with* us, did you check under the covers?"

"Haha, I think I would remember *that*." She said, swatting me once again. "Well…." She hesitated, and then pulled me in for a long slow hug. Her body was warm, and I instantly didn't want to leave.

"Have a nice walk…. I'll see you at work." She said, now pulling away.

I just smiled, leaving a hand on her arm for a moment, and walked away. Part of me wanted to dive right back in to bed with her, or offer to take her out to breakfast, father her children maybe, but I walked away.

I walked, and walked, and walked away. I may have even jogged a little, gotten a little lost, swore at the map on my cell phone a few times. That's the thing about walking away, it doesn't always go as planned. I had envisioned it as 'riding off into the sunset' (or sunrise in this case) but I quickly had to take it for what it was, and that was the infamous 'walk of shame'. I had always thought of this as something only a girl did, crying, with one broken shoe. Apparently the male version requires a map, and a brief stop off for a cheeseburger.

There was always a fleeting moment of fear whenever I found myself turning a corner to the place where my car *should* be. A bar parking lot is no stranger to temporarily abandoned vehicles, but for some reason I always had a slightly irrational fear that my vehicle was going to get towed away. Maybe it was a repressed fear of abandonment issue, which somehow manifested itself through my car.

With only minimal guidance from Google maps and a bad cheeseburger decision I found myself back at the infamous pub. Instead of the shock of turning the corner and *not* seeing my vehicle, I was confronted with something even worse, Jen! She was standing between my car and hers talking to a female I didn't recognize, but could only assume it was the long lost roommate.

For whatever reason, my immediate instinct was to dive right back around the corner as if I had run into unexpected gunfire. *Shit!* Talk about bad timing, there was literally no way for this to be a cool interaction. *Did she see me? Shit!* The only thing worse than awkwardly running right back into each other, was for her to have seen me dive back around the corner.

I stuck with my initial retreat decision with the full intention of denying the incident if I needed to later. I ducked into a little drug store just a few feet away, and apprehensively watched out the window. Thankfully it looked like I was in the clear. I watched Jen get into her car, and tried to sneak a better look at the roommate as she drove away.... just in case.

When the coast was clear, and the staff at the drug store stopped suspiciously staring at me, I finally reached my car, and a feeling of serenity. *What a night* I thought to myself. I wasn't sure if I had just established some well-earned bragging rights, or opened a can of worms that would make life at the hospital even more uncomfortable. Either way, what was done, was done, and there was no going back. I thought to myself, *maybe the hospital would offer some sort of discount on antibiotics, if the disease was contracted through a hospital employee?*

As amusing as I found myself, and my little accomplishment, it was time for a long overdue nap. I would need to be in top form now more than ever at work, the pressure was now on from every angle, most of it self-inflicted.

Chapter 8

"Regret for the things we did can be tempered by time, it is regret for the things we did not do that is inconsolable." –Sydney Smith

Waking up for my next shift at work filled me with *almost* as much anxiety as waking up next to Jen, only this time I knew where the bathroom was. The recent pressure of Gloria's fun filled little assignment, along with the added stress of having recently slept with a coworker made the idea of going to work very unappealing. *Was it too late to transfer to another unit?*

The thought of transferring stayed with me a little longer than it should have. What would I say, I'm sorry, but I would like to transfer to a unit where I haven't either pissed off, or had sex with anyone who works there? At this rate, I would probably run out of places to work before I learned how to avoid doing these things.

Unfortunately, I now had to get ready for my workday in the exact same way I would get ready for a date. I made sure my best scrubs were clean, a dash of cologne, (which is a no no in a hospital, it could effect fragile respiratory patients negatively, or just be obnoxious) I checked myself in the mirror obsessively, and came dangerously close to taking a 'pre-game' shot of whiskey to calm my nerves before walking out the door.

I had a tendency to spill something on my crotch before any big date, and this day was no exception. I had to slam on my breaks to avoid rear-ending someone who had slammed on *theirs* for no apparent reason, and spent the next 10 minutes nearly causing an accident myself, because I was now trying to wipe coffee off of my groin. This was a clear demonstration of the 'domino effect' in all of its glory, it was like paying it forward only backward. If we pay close enough attention, the universe loves to show us just how connected we really are, for better or for worse.

The hospital seemed a little more quiet than usual, something people in hospital culture were always quite suspicious of, even fearful, as if it was the calm before the storm. I wrote it off to the fact that I had arrived a little early to establish some sort of strategic advantage for whatever the day had in store. I wanted to be as prepared as possible for any professional, or personal curveballs. Ideally, the day would consist of minimal contact with Jen, and total avoidance of Gloria. My interactions with Jen would exhaustively put my social skills to the test. Professional distance had to be maintained, but not so much that it made working together weird. I would have to walk a tightrope between being a good coworker, and being the guy she just slept with, an inch off in either direction could wreak havoc on the other.

I couldn't help but wonder if women tortured themselves like this, or if only men felt this kind of pressure to be in control of every situation all of the time. Of course, I was unfortunately dealing with a Nurse, and hospital people are a different breed all together. Most of them had a kind, compassionate soul at one point in time, before it was crushed by the job, but exactly where Jen was in that process was difficult to determine. I had seen her in action during a code, and shrug it off like it was losing scratch off ticket, but I had also seen her go head to head against Gloria, which told me she had not given up fighting the good fight just yet.

Gloria had clearly lost it long ago, in more ways that one. They all seemed to have lost something along the way, something I felt like only a hospital could take away. The more experienced of the crew, Deets, Martha, and even Sylvia all shared an aura that is difficult to describe. It was as if they all were intimately aware of a solemn, or melancholy secret that they had to tell you, but didn't want to. Everyone on the planet knows something you don't know, but hospital people know something you don't want to know. Each deals with his or her sad secrets differently, some apparently eat them…. while some fizzle out and become robotic, concrete thinkers, just going through the motions. I couldn't help but wonder what would become of me, I could already feel myself more focused on just getting through my day unscathed than actually helping anyone in need.

I was taking a look at the white board in the back office, filled with names of patients written next to room numbers, followed by a diagnosis, a Doctor, a Nurse, and of course a billing code, when I felt someone come up behind me and give me a little hip-check. It was Jen, a little early, green protein shake in hand, and in all her glory.

"Hey stranger" she said

"Heeeey…. *Jen right?"* I said with a somewhat cocky grin.

"Ha ha, so its like that?"

"No, of course not, I'm just messing with you….I might still be a little drunk from the other night."

"Yeah, that was a bit rough"

Our conversation was cut short by the rest of the staff entering the room for the change of shift report before any real awkwardness could ensue. Jen sat next to me, people from the previous shift started with a passing disclaimer about how short staffed they were all night, before systematically going down the list of patients by room number and diagnosis, never their actual name.

They referred to each of them as only a numbered situation, or an assignment.... not a person. This is a way of speaking that is never formally taught in any medical terminology program, its just something that happens without anyone really ever even noticing.

We had our assignments, mine was kept light, not only because I was still new, but because Gloria had apparently already stepped in and made my little project known. Between my stumbling attempts to heal the sick, stave off death, and generally attempt to decipher the human condition, I had a researched report to write, designed to humiliate me, and downplay the significance of psychological wellness. *What could possibly go wrong?* At least Sylvia tried to carve out a little more time in my day for my extracurricular self-defeating activities. That was very nice of her. Sadly I could hear some staff grumbling about it under their breath, apparently in their eyes I had it too easy.

"Well have fun on your little project today." Jen smirked, this time only giving me a verbal hip check.

"Gee thanks"

"Oh don't worry, I suppose I could help you keep an eye on your patients if you need me to."

"Are you attempting to buy my silence? Or just irritate Gloria…. Either way it is greatly appreciated, but only partially necessary."

"I think it's a little bit of both, my presents alone is enough to irritate Gloria. I think she might have a little crush on you."

"Oh my dear Lord…. Are you *trying* to scar me today?"

"*Well,* you know how it used to go on the playground right? The kid that picked on you probably secretly liked you."

"Well if that's the case, then maybe I should have roughed you up, or pulled your hair a little earlier…." I said, already pushing the work boundaries I had planned to establish.

"Maybe you should have…." She said with a wink, and walked away perfectly.

Ooh that was good I thought to myself, *I'd let her have that one*. I just smiled as we went our separate ways. Normally I would have to steal the show in some way, and try to be the one to go out on a high note, but she was good, and deserved her moment. Besides, in my mind, the game was already over, and I had won.

I made a quick run down the hall, just to quickly introduce myself to my patients, even the ones that probably couldn't hear me. I always made it a point to try and talk to the ones everyone said were 'out of it', or 'comatose', just in case. This quick introduction also gave me an opportunity assess them for anything glaring that might come back to haunt me later, there was a good chance I may not even see some of them again during this shift. Nursing 101, *cover your ass*, the last thing you want is for a patient to be able to say, "I never even saw my nurse!"

From the initial glance it did look like I could be in for an easy shift, leaving me abundant time to work on my 'how to get fired and/or transferred' report in the office that time forgot. I was relieved for the moment, strangely calm considering my overall predicament. The few patients I had were stable, and seemingly content for the time being. I had what I considered a positive interaction with Jen, and had yet to even speak with Gloria, things were looking up.

I tried to ninja my way down the hallway, to my little office of doom, attracting as little attention as possible. I didn't want to have to explain the bizarre little task I was given, much less the one I actually planned on doing. Keeping any unintended human interfacing to a minimum was the key to my success.

As I was about to tread in to the darkened office with all the subtleties of James Bond, I caught a glimpse of a couple of semi-familiar faces down the hall. It was the hospital social worker Stacy and the Reverend I was introduced to the night Mr.Johnson died. Recognizing their faces was like a kick to the gut for some reason, like seeing the angle of death hovering around, it was just unsettling. I couldn't see the face of the person they were talking to, but judging by the fact that I could barely see them behind this person, it must have been Gloria, maybe they were just being absorbed by her gravitational pull.

Jen caught me peeking from the doorway and starting walking in my direction, instead of theirs. I could hardly blame her, they were like a negative energy vortex. I gave her a facetious look, and slowly backed up into the office, knowing she would follow. The two of us alone in an old abandoned office certainly had some possibilities, but I had to know what was going on.

"What is with the bad news band gathering down the hall?" I asked, as she strode into the room, far more gracefully than I ever could have managed.

"Oh, one of Gloria's patient is circling the drain." She said with almost shocking indifference.

"*Circling the drain huh*? Wow that was heartfelt, is that in the physicians reference book?" I said, smiling, trying not to show that I was actually a little disappointed by her absence of tact.

"Oh stop, you should be used to this place by now, you know I don't mean it like that. If I took every sad thing that happened here to heart I would have slit my wrists a long time ago."

"So should I prepare for a code?"

"No, she's got a few more months at least. The social worker is there with the family…. they just got her to sign a DNR, just in case."

"Oh, I see. I just get a little spooked when I see a social worker, a priest, and Gloria in close proximity."

"Well relax, they're not here for you…. Yet." She said with an unexpectedly sinister smile. For some reason even her ominous, not so indirect threat, was sexy to me. I knew she was attempting to be flirty and droll, but I couldn't help but wonder what her reaction would be if I was to find myself someday *'circling the drain'*.

"So…. Is this you and Gloria's little love nest?" She asked, looking around with disdain, slowly dragging her finger through the dust on the back of the office chair.

"Why yes, yes it is…. What do you think?"

"I think you can do better." She said with a wink.

"Better than Gloria, or better than this office?"

"Both."

"Oh I *have* done better, quite recently in fact...." I said, flashing my own sinister grin.

"Ok, ok, we better stop here before you say something stupid." She said, laughing, and giving me one of her signature swats across my shoulder.

She was right, it was only a matter of time before I pushed the conversation from a lighthearted exchange of witty banter, to an increasingly aggressive divergence, it was one of my many gifts to the world. I never knew where 'the line' was until long after I had crossed it.

"This is *indeed* my dusty little torture chamber where I am tasked to do Gloria's bidding." I said with a sigh.

"Well it could be worse, at least you're off the floor for a while."

"This is true, although I'm not sure where I would do the most damage to my career at this point."

"Oh, I think you'll be just fine…. I should probably get back out there, we don't want to start any rumors, now do we." She smiled, and strolled out of the room as eloquently as she had entered, sustaining eye contact until the last possible second. I realized as she was leaving that it was probably pretty obvious to the rest of the staff, at this point, that there was something more than a 'work relationship' happening here.

I decided to leave the door open just a little bit, to let in a few of the more distinguished sounds from the unit that I would likely need to pay attention to, codes, monitor alarms, desperate cry's for help, things of that nature. The computer seemed to struggle to 'boot up', it was as if it was choking on the same dust I was. The unanticipated delay gave me one last chance to contemplate what it was

I was doing in that room, a sliver of angst stuck in my side with the thought of Sylvia's reaction. Maybe I would say that I misunderstood the directions, that way they could just fire me for incompetence, instead of gross insubordination. I wondered which one would be easier to explain on a resume.

The computer screen finally lit up, making the dust floating in the air glow like miniature snowflakes. This would either be a gruesome scar on the face of my career, or a defining moment, thrusting not only myself, but the treatment of mental health patients entirely, a little further out of the dark.

I started digging through old charts as far back as the mid 90's when the hospital converted to an electronic record keeping system. This was actually somewhat impressive because most hospitals refused to convert to electronic record keeping, due to the cost, for nearly another decade. They only started switching over then, because their funding depended on it. Most states had regulatory agencies that proposed hospital funds would be cut unless they modernized their record keeping. Most hospitals waited until the absolute last second, modern clinical software systems, like everything else tied to our current healthcare system, cost millions of dollars.

No matter how much incriminating data I craved, there was no way I was going further back than the electronic records logged. Older information could only be found by sifting through actual paper files, buried deep within the hospitals core. Such a location would likely make the office I was currently in look like the Ritz-Carlton, and be somewhere between the morgue and a boiler room. I would likely have to search by candlelight, and fend off the occasional zombie.

I started compiling a list of patients admitted to the

medical unit that also carried a mental health diagnosis. I assigning numbers instead of names just like the hospital liked, although I did this for confidentiality and not callous depersonalization like the hospital does. I looked at the medications used, and the treatments they were billed for, in order to see if anything addressed their mental health needs. Not surprisingly, it looked like the vast majority of the patients were only treated for their medical concerns, while mental health needs were seemingly overlooked. The few cases in which a psychiatric medication was used, it was always a sedative. Typically short acting benzodiazepine like Ativan or Xanax. I had no doubt this was purely out of convenience for the staff, it was a way to shut them up, or even knock them out, at least until their shift ended. In nearly all of these cases, the doses were high enough to be considered a 'chemical restraint', although none were documented in that way.

This wasn't exactly the 'smoking gun' I was looking for, as horrendous as it was, it was hardly unexpected. In fact, I was quite convinced that this was probably happening on medical units all over the country. Mental health always takes a back seat to a patient's medical diagnosis, despite the growing body of evidence that the two go hand in had. Prominent modern-day studies have conclusively shown that the two are inseparable, despite resistance from the remaining lumbering dinosaurs like Gloria, who insist it is nothing but new age, hippie psycho-babble.

A report on this certainly wouldn't blow the lid off of the hospital, or even really surprise anyone who was acquainted with the matter, but that didn't change the fact that it needed to be done. I was left with a feeling of dissatisfaction, even finding what I was looking for wasn't enough, there was something missing, something wrong.

There was a nagging feeling in my gut that I could not escape, something sort of tugging at me. The way I found the room when Mr. Johnson died, the unanticipated death of Jen's patient Mrs. Barnett, and the suspiciously convenient DNR orders all seemed to lead down a murkier path. Not to mention the whole slow code thing, none of it sat well with me. I felt like that annoying character in a horror movie that was going to wander down that dark ominous path, no matter how loudly you yell at the screen.

With no shortage of personal risk, and complete disregard for my own career, I began digging into patient deaths. Not just their death, but anyone who had recent changes in their healthcare proxy, or fresh DNR orders. Because most of these patients did not carry a psych diagnosis, I had absolutely zero clearance to be looking at their files, and this was a big no no. In recent years personal privacy issues have come into focus more and more, as things like identity theft, and Medicaid fraud continue to make headlines. Sadly there are few things that will get you fired from a hospital faster than a HIPPA violation, but things like gross incompetence, perversion, and even the occasional murder, can glide safely under the radar without really ruffling anyone's feathers.

I held my breath through the first few files, not only because I was expecting red flashing lights and a HIPPA siren to go off, but because part of me was truly afraid of what I was going to find. My brief, self-induced stress apnea soon gave way to confusion when I discovered there wasn't just a correlation between hospital deaths, recent DNR orders, and changes with healthcare proxy's, but a direct unwavering connection.

I should have known, of course there was a connection between all of those things, how could there not be. When someone is nearing the end of their life, they have to make arrangements to ensure their wishes are carried out when there comes a point where they can no longer speak for themselves. Most people probably made tenuous arrangements long before they were ever needed, and therefore need to be updated, probably shortly before their deaths.

When a patient comes to terms with his or her mortal condition, and decide its time to move on, a DNR is predictably put in place while they wave the white flag. With this change in treatment philosophy, medication orders also tend to change and concentrate more on pain and comfort measures. On paper, every one of these events would naturally follow each other under standard conditions. This was a very frustrating realization, leaving my suspicions with essentially no paper trail whatsoever.

Just as I began to question my own sanity, another practice I had become very accustom to, I had a thought. *Why not be more specific?* I thought. Instead of searching for such broad coincidences, why not focus on exactly what, and *who* I was suspicious of. I started looking into the recent cases I had direct familiarity with, what staff had been assigned to them, and when.

Of course there was one name in particular my eyes were innately drawn to, Gloria, she had more patients die on her watch than almost anyone else. Early morning deaths, usually right at the beginning of the day shift, I could almost picture her smothering them with a pillow.

The dubious night shift squad had more than their fair share of patient deaths, but that too was to be expected.

Medically frail patients tended to die in their sleep, when their respiratory and circulatory systems slowed down. But there was a problem, the hand full of patients that had died under what I considered questionable conditions, didn't have a common denominator, they had two, Gloria and Martha.

Gloria had had each patient at some point during his or her hospital stay, and so did Martha. Gloria almost always had a hand in obtaining new DNR orders, but Martha had taken care each of the recent patients who had died within hours of their *actual* death. Could these two have been some kind of sadistic dynamic duo?

They were both ancient artifacts, severely lacking social skills, but this sort of malevolent teamwork went way beyond anything I could have predicted in my wildest nightmares. I sat back in my chair, letting my imagination run wild. *Gloria sets them up, and Martha knocks them down.... permanently*, I thought to myself. I had never actually seen them even speak to each other in person, but then again, there were probably those that could say the same about Jen and I. Maybe Gloria and Martha were *lovers*, two nasty old ladies doing 'the nasty'! *Holy shit, I'm finding new and exciting ways to even disgust myself* I thought, now questioning my sanity more than ever.

Before graphic images of Gloria and Martha getting it on could cause any significant brain damage, I interrupted by a knock on the door. I quickly changed screens on the computer with the speedy panic of someone looking at porn. It was Sylvia, she cautiously peeked through the door before almost tiptoeing in as if she was trying not to wake me up.

"Hey, how is everything going in here?" She asked gingerly, as if she was well aware of just how obnoxious the whole proposed little assignment was.

"Oh, it's going" I said, trying to be good-humored, not revealing my current level of alarm.

"Just *going?* I hope this isn't too much to take on right now, I wasn't quite sure when Gloria came to me about it. We did try and lighten your workload a little so you would have time for it today." She said.

"It's fine, I'm actually just wrapping things up right now." I said, opening up another window on the computer for additional camouflage.

"Oh good, I'm glad things seem to be going well for you here"

"Well…. It's been a learning experience for sure."

"If there is anything I can help you with just let me know."

"I will."

She started to turn toward the door, stopped, and

turned back. "Oh, I almost forgot to ask, I need to ask you for a small favor." She said, squishing her face up and trying to use her hands to make rudimentary 'small' gestures with her thumb and index finger.

"Shoot" I said, trying to not make it sound like *'shit'*.

"Is there any way you could stay a little late today? The night shift is short staffed tonight and I can't get anyone to come in until around midnight."

"I can probably do that" came out of my mouth before I had a chance to think it through. Apparently my desire to please people kicks into overdrive under stress.

"Oh thank you, you're a lifesaver! I think Gloria is going to stay a little over too just for some additional coverage for admissions."

Fuuuuuck! Seriously? I screamed in my head. Thankfully my mouth filtered it into "*Oh great*" for Sylvia's benefit.

Between that lovely piece of news, and trying to mask what I was actually doing in there, a tiny bead of sweat began to form and run down my forehead. I was afraid if she didn't leave at this point my head might explode, or at best a nosebleed.

"I really appreciate this David, I will let them know, thanks again and have a good night." She said, making her way out the door with her usual rapid exit fashion.

Gloria, the thought of her literally made me nauseous, and just as her name echoed down to my empty stomach, I had a unnerving realization. During my last conversation with Jen, she informed me that one of Gloria's patients was, as she put it, 'circling the drain'. New DNR orders were most likely already in place, setting the stage for part two of the dynamic death duo's disturbing routine. There was no denying it anymore, this was happening right in front of every ones eyes, hiding in plain sight, it was actually quite ingenious.

Part of me was undeniably in awe of their boldness, the sheer magnitude of what they were doing was truly epic. I couldn't help but wonder how it all got started. Was it planned? Were they talking over drinks one night, having a deep conversation about life, death, and their place in the world? (Maybe it was 'pillow talk' after a wild night of lesbian sex?) Was it pure evil, a game, just to see if they could get away with killing people? Why does anyone kill anyone, volumes could be written on the subject, and we would still likely never have a satisfactory, or universally accepted answer to that question.

The thought that stuck with me at the time is that this was all just an extension of the 'slow code'. A sane, logical person doesn't just jump into something like this, I imagine it as a more subtle slide. People under unimaginable stress, dealing with life and death on a regular basis, their will and their judgment eventually breaking down, trying to make sense of dealing with things that don't always make sense. Bending a rule, taking matters into your own hands, like with the slow code, vigilante style medicine is no doubt a slippery slope.

  I imagined it was like how anyone gets sick, the virus takes hold when the stress of the hospital already has them in a weakened condition, and they are more susceptible to such things. One day they believe they are being merciful, helping a patient die comfortably, the next day, taking them out before they can even make their own arrangements, or see their families. I could see how this all might have unfolded without much difficulty, it wasn't lurking in the shadows, it was right in front of every ones face, for those that would choose to see it.

For a moment I wished I could un-see it all, but I couldn't. The problem was that the setup was so cunning that proving it would be almost impossible, they would literally have to be caught in the act, and even then I wasn't so sure. There could even be more people involved, Deets, perhaps the entire night shift. I was suddenly starting to worry that I might be trapped in a really bad 'twilight zone' episode, and by the end of it I would be the latest recruit for the hospital from hell.

I was asked to stay late, this was an opportunity plopped in my lap. I had one advantage, and that was that they didn't know anyone was on to them. The disadvantages were many, I had no idea who might already know about this, or even be involved, and the minor detail of not actually having any idea what the hell I was going to do.

What I *did* know was that they most likely had a new

target, Gloria's patient who was 'circling the drain', little did he or she know they were about to get flushed like a goldfish won at a county fair. I couldn't let that happen, I would hide under the bed if I had to, it was time to do something right for a change. The old saying, 'those with the ability, have the responsibility' reverberated in my brain. To defend those who can no longer defend themselves is at the heart of our duty, not only as a Nurse, but also as a human being.

Chapter 9

"The idea is to die as young, and as late, as possible"

-Ashley Montagu

I couldn't dwell in self-righteousness forever, my dusty little office tomb had become just that, it was the place where nearly my entire shift had apparently come to die. I was likely needed out on the floor, and had to find a way to set up my little sting operation. Gloria was also staying over into the next shift, so she would most likely insist on keeping her doomed patient all to herself.

As I left my hiding place at the end of the hall I felt like a stranger on the unit now more than ever. But it was more than being a stranger now, it was worse; I was officially in enemy territory. I was James Bond and was following his playbook step by step, sleeping my way into the enemy's lair. Infiltration was complete, *in more ways that one,* I laughed to myself. For some reason the thought of Jen having any involvement seemed absurd, but when I saw her standing at the Nurse's Station I couldn't help but think to myself, *maybe I should sleep with her again.... just to make sure.*

"Heeey it lives!" Jen sarcastically exclaimed.

I put my hand up as if I was being blinded by the sun. "Jen.... Is that you? What day is it? How long was I gone?" I said with theatrical panache.

"Ugh, go back, you're still an idiot" She replied with matching zeal.

"Apparently I am, I volunteered to stay until midnight"

"Geez, if you're trying to dodge me just say so," she laughed.

"You're far too agile, and *flexible*, to dodge."

"Shh, you're an *ass!*" She said, trying to swat me as discretely as possible.

"Sylvia asked me if I could stay over a bit to cover the night shift. She lured me in by reminding me of how easy I had it today."

"Well you did have it easy, hiding in your little love nest with Gloria all day."

"Ugh, right."

"Well she was MIA for half the shift as well, sooo…."

"You're hilarious."

"I'm just saying." She said, flashing that incredible smile that started this whole thing. "Well do you need any help, I could probably stay over for a bit."

"No, that's ok…. I need some quality alone time with Gloria, we have some things we need to work out in our relationship." I said, attempting to flash my own wonderful smile, but no doubt paling in comparison.

"Ok well you have fun with that. Shoot me a text or something later."

"I will."

She turned and walked away, leaving her eyes on me as she turned, until the last possible second. I was too distracted to try and read into our conversation like I ordinarily would have done. I felt I had managed to successfully keep up my usual idiosyncrasies with her, despite my anxiety level. If there was one thing I excelled at, it was maintaining a substantial level of sarcasm in any situation.

Gloria vanishing for a portion of the shift came as no surprise, she was probably busy covering her *sizable* tracks. The night shift had already started gathering in the office for shift report and duty assignments, with Gloria still MIA there was a chance I could pick up her patient. I hurried into the back office, nearly knocking over Deets as I opened the door.

"Whoa, easy there sport, they'll all still be sick when

you get there." He said, regaining his balance.

"Sorry about that" I said, trying to help steady him without making too much man on man contact. What I really wanted to do was find an equivalently undermining nickname for every one of these crusty hospital people that referred to me as 'sport'.

"No harm no foul. We really appreciate you staying over for a bit, if you wouldn't mind just hanging on to the patients you had until relief gets here that would be great."

"Ah…. Sure, no problem."

I looked up at the assignment board and saw that Martha's name was written in along with Gloria's next to one of the patients. 'Rose Indigo' had the distinction of being the only patient they shared. DNR had been written in red after her name so recently I could almost smell the dry erase marker. The first step in my plan was already derailed.

Martha sat quietly in the back corner of the office writing down the details of her assignment. She couldn't possibly look more inconspicuous. I wondered if she had a subtle code, or short hand for her despicable plan, or maybe just wrote 'kill' after the names of patients with DNR orders. Why not throw something amusingly obvious into the whole thing, just to rub it in our faces.... I probably would have.

The good news was that my patient list from the prior shift was intentionally designed to be easy, allowing me time to work on my report. This gave me some wiggle room to keep my eye on Gloria and Martha's patient. Jen had presumably gone home, minimizing my opportunities for superfluous distraction. If it wasn't for the outlandish underlying circumstances, I might actually be bored for the first time sense I set foot on this unit.

Everyone eventually filed out of the office except for Deets. I could feel him watching me as I pretended to jot down a few last minute notes about my patients, trying to waste some time until everyone had completely dispersed and gone about their duties.

"So how is everything going?" He asked in a fatherly tone. A father that somehow knew his kid was up to something terrible.

"Its going" I said without looking up, attempting to appear enthralled in what I was writing.

"You just look a little stressed…. It seems like right about now is when new people either go back to where they came from, or quit all together." He said, sounding genuinely concerned.

"No no…. Its nothing like that, it's just been a very long day." I said, trying to sound reassuring even though the thought of going back to the psych unit had never sounded more appealing.

"Are you feeling like you have a better understanding now, for the way things are done on a medical floor?" He asked.

"Oh I definitely see how things are done around here." I said, making direct eye contact with a little more intensity than I probably should have.

"Ok.... Well just remember I'm here if you need me, we're all on the same team."

Are we? I thought, but didn't say anything out loud. There was an unexpected anger bubbling its way to the surface, and I found myself needing to take a step back from the conversation before I said something I might regret. Although I had no direct way to connect Deets to anything, there was no way he was ignorant of what was going on in this hospital. It was his teachings, his introduction to the slow code that first opened my eyes, and part of me hated him for it. If he had no moral hang ups about that, where did it end? For the time being, I would have to assume it didn't.

His little comment about being on the 'same team' made me wonder just how well I could really be maintaining my composure. It was time to try and fade into the background until I had an opportunity to catch Gloria and Martha in the act. My mission needed a code name; I was thinking, *My Big Fat Greek Nurse,* or *Unfree Willy....* Something to amuse myself while I attempted to intercept a hospital murder.

Unfortunately the only real way to hide on a medical unit was to utilize the illusion of being 'busy'. This was an art form in itself that I fortunately mastered during my many clinical rotations as a student nurse. Prolonging time in a medication room, storage closet, even the rooms of unconscious patients would effectively eat time away from a shift while always appearing to be hard at work. Some staff still favor the age-old 'disappearing act', but actually leaving the unit was too risky. In this particular case it would defeat the entire purpose of my mission. Ordinarily it is just a good way to rack up co-worker complaints and potential lawsuits.

Because of the nature of my undertaking I would have to use the least desirable of these methods to accomplish my objective, which was hiding out in an unconscious patients room. In what seemed like a rare lucky break, one of my mine was directly across the hall from the room I needed to see, the only problem was, she was far from unconscious. My strategically located patient was only in for a minor surgery and was scheduled for discharge in the morning.

Mrs. Macaroy, currently residing in room 347, had not so much made a peep in the last 12 hours, yet there she was, wide awake and completely coherent…. *Just Great* I thought. She was one of most picture perfect patients anyone could ever ask for, on any other night. This night, I was in need of a half dead one, or at least a deep sleeper.

"Hi Mrs. Macaroy, how are you feeling tonight?" I asked, trying to elongate the word *tonight*, even going as far as to let out a little fake yawn. I was hoping to employ a few subliminal psych tactics in order to get a sleeping pill into her.

"Oh I'm fine, don't worry about me hunny." She replied with all the comforts of my grandmother. (Hunny was better than 'Sport')

"Any pain, or…. Trouble sleeping?"

"Oh its not too bad hun, I'm going home first thing in the morning anyway."

"Yes indeed, big day tomorrow, I just wanted to make

sure you are rested up. And not *too* bad sounds like there *is* still some pain?" I said, reverting to playing up the pain side, some Percocet could probably do the trick just as nicely as a sleep aid.

"A little, but I can manage don't you worry." She said, still playing the sturdy grandmother.

"Well you should take advantage of your last night here, why don't you let me get you a little something for the pain so you can rest up for tomorrow?"

"Oh alright, I suppose." She conceded.

I would have felt guilty if I wasn't sure that she really was dealing with some pain. After all, this was probably the type of thing that got people like Gloria and Martha started in the first place, it was a slippery slope indeed. Given this woman's somewhat 'old school' personality, and the fact that she hadn't requested *any* pain medications following a cholecystectomy, I probably would have done the same thing in any given situation. Or so I told myself.

As I left for the medication room, I slowed my pace to prolong my look into the room across the hall. Rose Indigo's door was now partially shut. I glanced up and down the hall for unsolicited onlookers and slipped into her room. It had to have been Martha who last entered, no one had seen Gloria for hours. The only noise that could be heard was eerie sound of her ventilator, gently forcing her to breathe. It sounded like Darth Vader was taking a nap in the corner. Her monitors were still on, but the volume had been turned all the way down. She looked frail, her skin was paper-thin and almost an alien grey, except for the bruising from daily needle sticks. Looking at her like this made me wonder what she had been like a decade ago, a year ago, even days ago. I couldn't linger this close for too long, I had to keep my distance, both physically and mentally.

I made my exit as carefully as I had entered and continued to the medication room for Mrs. Macaroy's obligatory pain treatment. It was always an uncomfortable room for me to be in for some reason, I think it was because it smelled like a basement chemistry lab. It was easy to appear busy and hurried because I was, just not for the reasons anyone might expect, except perhaps Deets who I could feel watching from the Nurses Station as I left. I wasn't sure if he was somehow on to me, or if he just constantly had that 'I'm on to you' look on his face.

I slowed down again as I passed Indigo's room, I heard a noise almost like someone's cell phone. I peered in quickly but saw nothing out of place, her monitor volume had been turned back up, which seemed a little odd. I could hear someone walking up the hall so I ducked into my patient's room, nearly dropping her pain medications.

"Oh *hey* hun" she said, sounding wonderfully tired already.

"Hi, I've got you some pain medication, just relax and I'll push it right through your IV, you wont feel a thing." I whispered, still feeling a little creepy about the whole thing.

"Oh good, thank you, it was starting to hurt me a bit more."

Thank God I thought as I pushed the plunger on the syringe, now feeling a great deal better about myself. The effect was almost immediate, she adjusted herself in her bed a little bit as I slowly cleaned up my supplies. I could hear her breathing relax and slow down as she fell asleep, there was an inexplicable sense of peacefulness about it. I now had my lookout point, and there was a peculiar sense of peacefulness about that as well.

My peace however, was destined to be short lived. I had no sooner taken a deep breath in an attempt to slow my own breathing when it happened. I heard the swish of loosely fitting scrubs in the hall, followed by the creak of the door across the hall. My heart fluttered as I stood frozen in Mrs. Macaroy's darkened room. I strained to hear some indiscernible sounds from Indigo's room as I creped closer to the door. The quick sound of a switch flipping could be made out among the discreet rustling. Just then, an earsplitting alarm shrieked from inside of the room.

This was it, I started to dart across the hall only to be cut off, and nearly knocked over, by Gloria, who seemed to come out of nowhere. She didn't even look at me as she stormed into Indigo's room. She hastily shoved the door open and flicked on the lights exposing Martha next to the bed, frozen like a deer in headlights. She had the ventilator power plug in her hand, the alarm still blaring that had been triggered by the loss of power.

"*Martha!*" Gloria shouted, grabbing the power cord and slamming it back into the wall outlet.

"Gloria, I was just…."

"You were just what, what Martha? Caught off guard by the alarm you had turned down earlier?"

Other monitor alarms were still beeping and buzzing as Indigo's heart struggled to manage the recent oxygen cut off. I looked, and her IV Morphine was now running wide open, I quickly reached past them both and clamped the IV line.

"What the fuck is going on here?" I asked, looking at Gloria with legitimate confusion.

"Nice touch Martha…. Crank up the Morphine and let it finish your work." Gloria said, inching closer to Martha who was clearly caught completely off guard.

"I have no idea what you're talking about" Martha murmured, and tried to make her way to the door.

"You know exactly what the fuck I'm talking about Martha." She said, blocking her exit. "I've been watching you for years, I'm just sorry it took me till now to catch your crazy ass! I followed you tonight, and turned the alarm back up after you had turned it down, I wanted to hear you do it for myself."

"Do what, I haven't done anything wrong!" She shouted, tears now running down her cheeks.

Just as Gloria looked like she was about to physically pounce on her, the alarm tones intensified, signaling a cardiac arrhythmia, Indigo was in trouble. Other staff started descending on the room in response to the alarms, and no doubt all of the shouting.

"What's going on in here?" Becky snapped as she rushed into the room. "*Shit*, call a code!"

Deets followed in closely behind, as Martha managed to slip out, just as he entered the room.

"Hold on, hold on." He said, steadily putting his hand on Becky's shoulder.

"But she's flat-lining!" Becky said, trying to mask her trepidation.

"She's a DNR…. Just turn off those alarms, its all we're suppose to do…. Its all we *can* do at this point." Deets said calmly.

"Under the circumstances, shouldn't we do something? Martha turned the vent off and gave her an overdose of Morphine!" I said.

"Now hold on, what happened?" Deets said, looking like he was only pretending to be stupefied.

"You know Goddamn well what happened and what's *been* happening!" Gloria roared.

"Hold on!" He stammered.

"No you fucking hold on! She might be DNR, but she was overdosed on Morphine, we can treat that!" I said, no longer able to control, or mask my anger.

"Counteracting the Morphine wont do anything now, and neither would running a code…. Do you want to get sued?" He replied, maintaining an astounding level of poise.

"He's right…. he's right…." Gloria said, holding her hands up in the air as if she was surrendering, and she was. We all were, what choice did we really have now. Rose Indigo was gone.

Chapter 10

"Our lives begin to end the moment we become silent about things that matter."

–Martin Luther King Jr.

We all stood in silence, for what seemed like an eternity, but was probably less than a minute. Our body language still engaging in the final blows of the battle, but there was nothing left be said. Indigo's body lay lifeless, but with the vent still running after Gloria plugged it back in, it looked like she was still breathing.

Martha despondently walked over and turned off all of the machines, filling the room with a silence that seemed even louder than the alarms. One at a time everyone left the room, and headed in their own directions. Becky and I were the last lingering, we both just stared at the body.

"Go ahead…. I'll clean up in here." She said.

I walked out without saying anything in return. It was not out of impoliteness, and she knew that, I was just in a mental state that would not allow anything but emotion to come through, and the only emotion readily available at the time was anger. I had failed, not only to intervene and save a life, but I had failed to discover a would-be ally in a battle I didn't realize was already underway.

I had underestimated Gloria in the worst way possible. It was humbling, we did have our irretrievable differences, but I had misjudged her as a person. Despite her hardened, and sometimes seemingly shortsighted methods, her mission was still the protection of life, and she was doing it the only way she knew how. She had been one step ahead of me, and two steps ahead of Martha the whole time. I would love to insert a fat person joke, but since I had just basically had my ass handed to me by one, the joke was on me.

There is nothing quite like being knocked down a peg, it is an experience I highly recommend. It doesn't matter how it happens, just as long as it does once in a while, it seems to make a person reevaluate not only themselves, but their place in the world. My place in the hospital world was forever changed, there was no turning back, nothing could be unseen or unsaid. It was like I had broken something that could never really be put back together the same way, instead of trying to glue it back together, I felt like breaking it some more, so it would fit neatly into the garbage.

While imagining a garbage can large enough to climb into, I discovered that I was virtually alone on the unit. Martha, Gloria, and Deets were all nowhere to be found. Martha I expected to be MIA, crying in a bathroom, or planning a flight to a country without extradition laws. But the other two's whereabouts were a mystery, one I didn't have the time or the energy to solve. My days of playing Scooby-Do in the hospital were over. But there was one last order of business that I needed to finish, there was a report expected from me, the hospital had mistakenly given me a microphone and I intended to use it.

It what can only be described as a true 'fuck it' moment, I marched right back into my dusty little office dungeon, slammed the door, and locked it. I didn't bother opening up the hospitals clinical software or medical records, just a word document, that was all I needed. I titled the document simply, "An Overview of Treatment". Such a brief title gave it a boldness that I was prepared to run with. It went a little something like this:

'The overall treatment of patients in this facility falls exceedingly short of any established markers that measure success. During my recent research into the

treatment, and staff coverage of psychiatric patients being treated for medical conditions, it became clear that there was a level of dysfunction that reached far beyond anything I could have predicted.

There is a sickness in this hospital, one that affects every patient, staff, or visitor that comes through its doors. A systemic disease that did not get its start here, it began as a result of a healthcare system that is designed as a business model. One that focuses on how a profit can be made from the misfortune or illness of others.

We live in one of the only developed nations on Earth where cost of treatment is the number one concern when a person falls ill. Money will literally decide whether a person lives or dies. Insurance companies who have never laid eyes on the patient will make the treatment decisions, not the Doctor. As a healthcare professional, the vast majority of my efforts and documentation, surround billing, and the avoidance of lawsuits, instead of patient care.

This arrangement has caused an infection that has spread into every aspect of our healthcare system, and manifested itself in this facility in the worst ways imaginable. Short staffing due to budget cuts (saving money) has lead to crushing workloads, and strained staff both mentally and physically. The care of someone whose very life is in danger has an inherent level of stress that few can sustain. Seeing death first hand on a daily basis withers away on psyche of even the most hardened medical professionals.

In this facility, the virus has spread to its very soul. Some of our most trusted staff members are now willing to purposely cut a patients life short, for what they no doubt believe is for the greater good. They have forgotten what their very purpose was, and become a part of the machine. A healthcare machine that only holds on to a patient until every dime has been squeezed out, then cuts them loose to make room for the next cash cow.

The staff here is willing to make life and death decisions for a complete stranger in order to accommodate their own conveniences. They have found ways to justify ignoring the last wishes of both the patient and their families. They have found ways to justify ignoring the very oaths they swore to uphold. They have traded in their morals in order to cope with the misguided demands of our vile healthcare machine.

The irony of being asked to evaluate the care we provide our psychiatric patients with on a medical unit is flabbergasting. The people charged with the care of someone with mental health needs have vastly more severe psychiatric problems than the patients they are supposed to be taking care of.

It is my professional opinion, that there is no real treatment taking place in this facility, there is only the illusion of treatment. The patients literally trust their lives to people who are no longer worthy of trust. Although not all here are guilty of the actions I have described, most are guilty of turning a blind eye. As a result of my research, I have no choice but to recommend that a full investigation be launched into every patient death that has occurred on these grounds, and that every employee undergo extensive training in stress management, and ethics. I plan to report my findings to the joint commission and governing body, and resign from this facility, effective immediately.'

So there it was, one big steaming pile of a report, along with a surprise resignation. Hell, the resignation even surprised *me*, but what else could I really do. I compiled a list of oversight committees, abuse and even fraud hotlines to tell my story to. (Well, not the *whole* story, I left out the gratuitous sex scene and fat jokes) I made sure even a local media group got a hold of the story.

As a result of actions I was not privy to, Martha was reportedly offered a transfer to another facility, but chose to resign instead. I had heard later that Deets resigned as well, and moved out of the healthcare field entirely. There were never any criminal charges filed on anyone's behalf, or even a lawsuit, surprisingly enough. The whole thing was sort of just absorbed by the hospital. I heard a rumor that a new form had to be signed with any new DNR order, and that a new 'ethics' portion was added to the new employee orientation program.

In the end, I definitely didn't change the world, or even make a dent. But when I chose to derail my own career for the greater good, I did something else; I found a new use for myself. My world changed for the better, as did my place in it. I managed to stay in healthcare, but no longer work in a hospital setting. I have since settled into both community health, and a teaching role, which is probably as terrifying for my subordinates as it is for me. But if I can simply open a few eyes, my exploits have not been in vein.

As for Jen, and my more personal adventures…. well, that's another story….